HOME SCHOOLING
Answering Questions

ABOUT THE AUTHOR

Kerri Bennett Williamson is a free-lance writer, artist, designer, and instructor; who is busily involved in the home schooling movement. Utilizing the integrated holistic learning approach, she has been continuing her education since graduating from high school. By those who know her, she is considered to be well educated in many areas of study.

She and her husband are parents of four children (aged two, four, six and thirteen) and have been home schooling for five years. Kerri served as newsletter coordinator and editor (three years), and a director (one year) for H.A.N.A. (Homescooler's Association of Northern Alberta). As an individual who is active in her community, she often shares of her knowledge pertaining to home schooling.

HOME SCHOOLING
Answering Questions

By

KERRI BENNETT WILLIAMSON

CHARLES C THOMAS • PUBLISHER
Springfield • Illinois • U.S.A.

Published and Distributed Throughout the World by

CHARLES C THOMAS • PUBLISHER
2600 South First Street
Springfield, Illinois 62794-9265

© 1989 by CHARLES C THOMAS • PUBLISHER

ISBN 0-398-05615-3

Library of Congress Catalog Card Number: 89-5104

With THOMAS BOOKS *careful attention is given to all details of manufacturing
and design. It is the Publisher's desire to present books that are satisfactory as to their
physical qualities and artistic possibilities and appropriate for their particular use.*
THOMAS BOOKS *will be true to those laws of quality that assure a good name
and good will.*

Printed in the United States of America
SC-R-3

Library of Congress Cataloging-in-Publication Data

Williamson, Kerri Bennett.
    Home schooling : answering questions / by Kerri Bennett
Williamson.
        p. cm.
    Bibliography: p.
    Includes index.
    ISBN 0-398-05615-3
    1. Home schooling—United States—Miscellanea. I. Title.
LC40.W55 1989
649'.68—dc20   89-5104
                                                                CIP

To families in our future.
For what is our future,
without families.

INTRODUCTION

As an individual involved in parenting, community, and home schooling organizations, I have frequently been asked questions about home schooling. Uncounted hours of mine have been donated to friends, acquaintances, and strangers alike, in the answering of questions about this little known educational alternative.

When those interested in home schooling have called to quiz me, I have been faced with two choices: to answer their questions for a few hours, therefore losing a hefty chunk of my valuable day; or to tell them to go read some books on the subject, which was less than I wanted to offer.

I felt forced into finding a solution to this dilemma in order to save my time for: personal, marital, and family pursuits; the nurturing, guiding, and teaching of our four children; and work within our family business. My desire to help others gave me the incentive to compile an information kit: a small selection of articles and recommended book titles. I was eventually dissatisfied with this, as it would not have been sufficient for me when I first inquired about home schooling, and it wasn't satisfactory for those who inquired of me about home schooling. They still asked me questions.

As a plan to perfect my *introduction to home schooling* kit, I began to jot down the many questions people confronted me with and the answers that I provided to them. My efforts to prepare a small handout for inquirers of home schooling sparked a fire that grew into that which begged for book form. I decided to succumb.

Ten years ago I heard about home schooling and knew not where to turn, what to read, nor who to quiz. Six years later I stumbled upon people who, and books wherein, I was able to obtain answers to many of my questions. My research was exhaustive and answers to my questions were not always easily obtained. By writing this book in a question-and-answer format, I felt that answers to questions could be found more easily. Those who have embarked upon the home schooling quest will find that this book will enable them to uncover particular information they seek.

Although I have my own personal ideas, beliefs, and feelings about the ideal home school, I have focused predominately on providing information about home schooling and related subjects in general. However, I occasionally share my personal philosophies.

When I first looked for the answers to my home schooling questions, I was searching for a book such as this one, and it is my hope that this book will help others who are searching for what I have found.

CONTENTS

HOME SCHOOLING
Answering Questions

ANSWERING QUESTIONS

1) I have heard that home schooling is illegal. Is it legal or not?

Home schooling has always been a legal educational alternative. Across the United States and Canada, there are varying allowances made for home schoolers. Some states (provinces) are very rigid and others are extremely flexible in cooperating to support home schooling opportunities. School acts have always provided for alternatives in education, and policies are generally readjusting to accommodate the rapidly increasing numbers of home schooling families.

In some states (provinces), schooling authorities and teachers are very cooperative with home schooling families. Recognized as an excellent alternative form of education, there is often effective support, allowing home schooling students to implement ideally individualized programs.

In many instances, home schooling families find little or no cooperation from educational authorities and end up in a kind of *limbo state*, where they are trying to work out a mutually acceptable situation. This *shopping around* for a principal or superintendent can last quite some time, sometimes years. Because of this, many parents who begin by trying to work with authorities end up home schooling independent of the public system.

Although there are many families who home school without permission from state (provincial) authorities, these families insist that this is not illegal. The law infers that children must be receiving efficient instruction, in public or private schools, in the home or elsewhere.

Cases in which the home schooling parents take complete responsibility of their children's education, without cooperation or even strong opposition from local authorities, have been tried in the courts and most families have won. Judges have concluded that these children are indeed receiving an equal education at home and, more often than not, a far superior education than could be provided at an institutional school.

Unfairly, home schooling families are often expected to prove that their children are receiving efficient instruction and an adequate education. Many home schooling parents believe that the onus should be placed on the *authorities* to prove that their children would indeed be receiving a superior education in an institutional schooling situation.

The institutional school is assumed by most to be providing an adequate education. How, then, do the institutional schooling authorities account for the increasing numbers of failing children, year after year after year? How can the authorities claim an adequate education is provided? Material is being taught but not always learned. Perhaps *failing* is deemed adequate by the institutional schooling authorities. It is the *institutional school* that should be on trial.

(See Donn Reed's *The First Home School Catalogue* for an idea of what states and provinces accommodate home schoolers and in what way; and John Holt's *Teach Your Own* for more information on legalities.)

2) Home schooling is just a recent fad, right?

Home schooling is an old educational standard and is now a growing trend because of renewed interest in this superior form of education. Many who have been reared in the *public school era* do not realize that home schooling has actually been around much longer than *state-imposed* institutional schooling. Studies by Hewitt Research unveiled that at the beginning of this century, on this continent, a very small percentage of children (approximately 10%) attended public school. This percentage increased until the early fifties, when the peak enrollment was at it's highest (approximately 90%). The public school *monopoly* has declined to 75 percent or less since that time.

Renewed interest in home schooling has substantially increased the percentage of the populous now involved. At the present time, enrollment in the public schools declines each year, while the numbers of home schooling students are steadily increasing. It is not reasonably possible to determine how many children are home schooling, since so many families are doing so independent of and unregistered with the public school systems. Researchers have concluded that there are, however, possibly one million known home schoolers in the United States alone.

It is widely accepted amongst home schooling advocates that there are many more unregistered home schoolers than those who are registered with government schooling boards. The greater numbers of independent home schoolers can be attributed to the lack of cooperation of most institutional schooling systems. Many home schoolers begin with a desire or conviction to work with the *authorities*, but few parents find the freedoms they feel they have rights to in the exercise of educating their own children.

Schooling authorities need to acknowledge the rights of the individual and then their own responsibility and purpose: to serve individuals by aiding parents in the education of their children. A climate conducive to good relations between parents and schools must be established by the schools.

3) Aren't home schooling parents rebellious?

Parents who home school their children may be considered rebels. They rebel against infringement upon their freedoms. They rebel against those who would take away their rights to raise, nurture, and educate their own children. They rebel against those who would create acts or bylaws that deviate from the original law, the law that was designed to protect the rights of the individual. They rebel against a low standard of education for their children.

Henry David Thoreau has said, "Unjust laws exist . . . shall we be content to obey them or shall we endeavor to amend them, and obey them until we have succeeded, or shall we transgress them at once? . . . The ways which the State has provided for remedying the evil . . . take too much time, and a man's life will be gone."

Parents who choose home schooling are those who usually refuse to watch their children destroyed, hurt, or otherwise damaged by unjust laws while the needed amendments may or may not be effected during the schooling years of their children. Hopefully, there will be more and more enlightenment in the future; that succeeding generations will have more freedom of choice through the laws and bylaws.

Some home schoolers feel that the *camel in the tent* parable is somewhat applicable here. There was a man who owned a tent and a camel. One windy night, the camel sought to enter the tent and inquired of the man as such. The man said that there was not room in the tent for the both of them, but he conceded to let the camel put his nose in. The camel pressured for more and more, until the camel was fully in the tent and had shoved the man out. What was originally the man's servant became his master, and what was rightfully owned by him was stolen by the camel. The man became the servant.

These home schoolers believe that individuals are the *man*, education is the *tent*, and the government is the *camel*. This moment in time just may be crucial as far as securing our rights and freedoms go. We must insist on all that is and should truly be ours as individuals, rather than begging for a little here or a little there. The governmental body has already become more and more our master in many areas of concern, because individuals have conceded to let the government put its nose into our daily lives more and more. Yes, the government can provide tents for those who need shelter, but no individual should be shoved out of a tent that is rightfully his or hers.

Some parents may believe that the government is the *man,* education is the *tent,* and individuals are the *camel.* These people are content to bow down to the government for the most part and just plea and bargain for a little here and a little there. They beg to put their nose into the tent, hoping perhaps that someday they will accomplish the great task of obtaining the tent.

Parents who home school their children believe in upholding their individual freedoms and rights, and they uphold the original law that was designed and created to protect their individual rights. They seek after a high standard of education for their own children and hope for the same, eventually, for all children.

Those who believe in and are willing to fight for the right to home school children tend to be those who believe in and are willing to fight for all individual rights and freedoms. True individual rights and freedoms can be won by working for the rights of the individual while recognizing the needs of the group as a whole.

The United States and Canada are *still* free countries for the most part, and the people of these countries must speak out for existing freedoms to be maintained, past freedoms to be regained, and new freedoms to be attained. When changes need to be implemented, the people must stand up and *vote* or their *vote* will be taken away from them. The governments *by the people, for the people,* are gradually becoming the governments *over the people for the government.*

Groups of people banded together to abolish slavery. Citizens lobbied to secure the vote for every man and woman. Workers stood together to improve conditions. Couples spoke up to naturalize birth. Individuals must rise up to abolish the unjust, secure individual rights, improve working and living conditions, and naturalize life and learning.

These *rebels* have a just cause and will fight for true freedom for those rights that they believe they are entitled to, just as our ancestors did in order to secure the freedoms we now enjoy.

4) I've read about some very irresponsible home schooling parents. Are most of them like that?

A few highly publicized cases of irresponsible home schooling parents have caused undo criticism of home schooling parents in general. One bad apple can give the whole barrel a bad name.

The three most common myths about irresponsible or even abusive home schooling parents are: the fanatically freakish religious parents who *save* their children from all secular knowledge by using only *their Bible* as the curriculum; the cruel slave-driving parents who keep their children home from school in order to *exploit* them through work in fields, factories, and otherwise; and the constantly booze-drunk or drug-stoned parents who are so *oblivious* to reality that they don't bother sending their kids to school.

Very few home schooling parents are religious freaks. Although many home schooling families have religious and/or moral beliefs, few of them home school solely for religious reasons. These parents home school their children because they truly believe this form of education to be in the best interests of their children, their community, their country and even the world.

Home schooling parents seldom use their children as slave labor. All parents have opportunity to abuse their children in whatever way and this is always a tragedy. Home schooling parents are no more and probably less likely to abuse their children than the average parent. Some home schooling parents work with their children on family projects and businesses as an integral and practical part of their education.

Very few home schooling parents are drunken, drug-junkie hippies. The vast majority of home schooling parents are conscientious, responsible, and determined to provide not only quality education but loving nurturing and healthful food for their children. It is precisely because these parents care that they go to the effort of taking on the responsibility of educating their own children.

5) **What kind of parents home school their children and are they all doing it for basically the same reasons?**

Whether or not they choose to home school or institutionally school their children, parents could be divided into three general groups: parents who *love* their children; parents who are *apathetic* towards their children; and parents who *dislike* or even *hate* their children.

It is possible that there are parents who home school their children for reasons other than that they care greatly for and love their children. There are the few exceptions to the rule. It is possible that a select few *home schooling* parents are apathetic to or even dislike their children, but what would it profit an apathetic or hateful parent to keep their children home?

Parents who don't care would not go to any trouble to educate their children at home. Parents who dislike their children would sooner get rid of their children by sending them to an institutional school. It is much more likely that home schooling parents love their children. This does not infer that non-home schooling parents do not love their children.

Parents who send their children to institutional school do so usually because they think that it is best for their children. There are those parents, though, who are apathetic or dislike their children, are glad to get rid of their kids during institutional school hours, and dread the weekends, holidays and summers, when their children will be home for extended periods of time.

For those loving parents who send their children to school because they think it best for them, as the children become older it usually becomes increasingly difficult to care about and love their children, who have gradually become strangers to them because of such constant separation.

Parents who find themselves loving their children less will often feel guilty for feeling this way. These parents may not recognize that it is the separation of parents and children which causes these pulled-apart feelings and not anything in particular that the parents themselves did wrong. Parents of institutionally schooled children should not feel guilty for the family breakdown that has occurred, when they did not know that institutional schooling would cause this generation gap.

Those parents who learn of home schooling well into the institutional schooling of their children will often react with an *it's too late* feeling or a *defensive* attitude. If they can get past these feelings of fear and guilt, they can tackle the challenge of home schooling.

Because many people have an *old dog* attitude, they are afraid of or resist learning new *tricks*. People with a *pioneer* attitude are usually more resilient and readier for change or progress. For this reason, the *young in thought* are more often to embark upon a home schooling trek.

Most parents who home school their children fall into the group of parents who love their children. These parents care about and love their children enough to take an active part in the education of their own children. They home school their children because they believe that it is the best education they can provide for them.

Within the group of loving parents who home school, there are three basic reasons for so doing: as a cure to institutional school damage; as an exercise in individual responsibility; and/or as an effort to allow for natural learning to take place.

The parents who are looking for a cure feel that the institutional school has inflicted *diseases* upon their children. These parents *pull out* their failing, depressed or otherwise troubled children from the institutional school in order to save their children from further damage.

Others simply believe in taking on the responsibility for their childrens' educations. These people believe in the *individual* over the *state* and that they have a fundamental right to exercise their own decisions, based upon their own consciences, instincts, intuitions and feelings.

Many parents who have a *natural attitude* towards education home school their children to allow nature to takes its course for the most part. They feel that the institutional classroom and its *structured, scheduled, systematic schooling* is a hindrance to real learning.

Many home schooling parents find upon meeting each other that they share parallel thinking in many other areas of thought. It is quite common for home schooling parents to be *in* to such things as home birth, home businesses, healthful eating, preventative and natural medicine, environment and animal protection, and other less than recently traditional ideas.

6) **I'm concerned about the children whose parents would experiment on them by home schooling. Shouldn't the government step in to protect these kids?**

The general public may view home schooling as an experiment in a new form of education, but home schooling is a proven theory, a tried-and-true educational alternative. In truth, institutional schooling is an experiment in a relatively new form of education, the unproven theory.

From the beginning of recorded history, parents have taught their own children in and around their homes and workplaces. *Home schools* have successfully stood the test of time. In a broad sense, all parents are *constantly* experimenting with their children in one way or another, but, barring harmful neglect or abuse, *parents have this right.* The government should not have the right to *take over* in situations where the parents wish to retain responsibility in any area of their children's lives.

The majority of parents home school or have home schooled their children. At least the first year or first few years of children's lives are spent in their homes being taught various things by their parents. Many parents place their children in the *hands* of others to teach and care for (institutional schools, day-cares, baby-sitters, nannies), but *home schooling parents* choose to continue teaching and caring for their children, personally.

Home schooling parents are concerned about the vast experiment of the institutional schools and for the children who are herded off to institutional school like cattle to the stockyards.

Home schooling advocates are concerned for the children who are given to governments, or any other organization, as guinea pigs in worldwide experimentation, which tends to suppress the occurrence of genius and consistently suppresses the self-esteem, self-motivation, individuality, and creativity of the children who are so constrained to be experimented upon.

Beyond dissatisfaction with the differing methods of education and evaluation utilized by institutional schools, proponents of home schooling are deeply concerned over certain elements in curriculums that portray crude language, homosexuality, nudity/pornography, sexual promiscuity, abortion as contraception, violence, and socialism as acceptable.

Some sexual education classes cause many parents to worry: girls are taught that the best safeguard against unwanted pregnancy is lesbianism, and abortion is just contraception; kids are taught not only that condoms will save them from AIDS and other sexually transmitted diseases but they are encouraged to be *normal* and freely experiment sexually; at early ages, children are told about masturbation and are made to feel *abnormal* if they don't do it frequently; sexually explicit films are shown.

Many parents who's personal beliefs are not compatible with such *teachings* have found that changing the school curriculum is a tough nut to crack. Some parents decide not to try to make the best of this bad situation; rather, they decide to remove themselves from it by choosing to take the education of their children into their own hands.

Many home schooling parents feel that not only does *a picture speak a thousand words* but a picture can leave an *impression* that will *last* a thousand years. These parents believe in the importance of keeping certain *pictures* from their children's minds in order to protect the present and future of their children.

These morally protective parents also feel that there is wisdom in carefully choosing written material for their children to read. As Ezra Taft Benson has said, "It is the mark of a truly educated man to know what not to read." If being selective in one's reading is censoring, then there is a need to censor.

Theodore Roosevelt once said, "To educate a man in mind, and not in morals, is to educate a menace to society." William Howard Taft, another president of the United States, said, "Unless education promotes character making, unless it helps men to be more moral, more just to their fellows, more law abiding, more discriminatingly patriotic and public spirited, it is not worth the trouble taken to furnish it."

John Ruskin has said, "Education does not mean teaching people what they do not know. It means teaching them to behave as they do not behave. It is not teaching the youth the shapes of letters, and the tricks of numbers, and then leaving them to turn their arithmetic to roguery, and their literature to lust. It means on the contrary, training them into the perfect exercise and kindly continence of their bodies and souls. It is a painful, continual, and difficult work, to be done by kindness, by watching, by warning, by precept, and by praise, but above all by example."

A home schooling father and advocate, Reed A. Benson, has said, "Character sees further than intellect." This phrase illustrates that although intellectual training is of import, character building is of far greater importance.

As a poet once penned:

Men are blind until they see, that in the human plan,
Nothing is worth the building if it does not build the man.
Why build these cities glorious, if man unbuilded goes?
In vain we build the world unless, the builder also grows.

What worries many parents is that not only are their children not being taught proper morals in institutional school but that they are actually being taught anti-morals.

A less apparent happening than *immoral* teachings, but a concern to those who recognize it, is the subtle *undermining* of parental authority. Often with good intentions but sometimes in direct defiance against the parents of their students, teachers tell their students to disregard the teachings of their parents. Children are often told to go home and tell their parents to *buckle up, stop smoking,* and other well-meant messages. The problem lies in the deliverance of the messages. Teaching children that it is their right to go home and tell their parents to smarten up and do this or that is undermining parental authority.

Frequently encouraged by teachers, children keep secrets from their parents, secrets like what they learned in class about sexual things and how they really feel about private things. Teaching children that it is their right to keep secrets that are none of their parents' business anyway is undermining parental authority.

Even if the previous *moral* concerns and problems could be addressed and remedied, many parents believe that the basic removal of children from their family homes for their education is not justified nor wise. Family *interdependence* and *dependence* upon siblings and parents is replaced by institutional interdependence and dependence upon peers and teachers. Many individuals see this as a weakening of the family and ultimately the society, because the family unit is the basic structural unit of society.

A government that steps in to take control of the education of children is one that is turning those children into *children of the state.* Karl Marx wrote that one of the first steps to bringing a country to communism is bringing the children to public school. Many home schooling advocates believe that there is a very real change occurring in North America, from democracy to socialism.

Whether or not this change is being brought about deliberately by people with power or through a gradual unorganized evolution, this change must be reversed. It is apparent to many that constitutional rights of the individual and his or her needs are being smothered by the rights of the *state* and its needs.

Although they feel justifiably concerned, home schooling parents claim no right to force or coerce parents of institutionally schooled children to do as they do. They allow other parents the privilege and the right to educate their children as they see fit and expect to be allowed the same freedoms of choice by family, friends, acquaintances, and the government.

7) **How do home schooling children receive proper socialization, like average kids at school?**

Surprising to many, desired proper socialization is the prime reason for a majority of home schooling parents to join this uncommon but growing trend. While it is true that home schooled children are not *socialized* as average institutionally schooled children are, most home schooling parents believe that home schooling nurtures natural socialization.

Home schooled children socialize naturally with family members, neighbors, and acquaintances of all ages, resulting in a natural, well-rounded socialization. Standard tests of social adjustment, such as the *Piers-Harris Children's Self-Concept Scale*, have found home schooled students on top. Home schooled children are socially confident and well adjusted.

Comparatively, institutionally schooled children are conditioned by the schooling situation into interacting almost exclusively with same-aged peers. It is the belief of most home schoolers that institutionalized schooling actually guarantees the child an education in anti-social behavior. Few children escape the deleterious effects of institutionalized schooling's *anti-socialization*. Studies have shown that the excess peer group association that institutionalized schooling *provides* promotes unnatural peer dependence and *negative* sociability. Institutionally schooled children are socially insecure and maladjusted.

Our society in general has become conditioned into believing that the behavior of institutionally schooled children is normal. This average behavior is common, simply because the average child is commonly schooled institutionally. The behavior of the average child is common but unnatural and unhealthy.

Home schoolers defend the theory that home-centered socialization is superior to institution-centered socialization, particularly for young children. Home schooling parents defend their rights to provide their children with home-centered socialization. The original laws surrounding education were instituted to ensure an equal opportunity to a quality education. These laws were not instituted to ensure institution-centered socialization.

John Holt (a high-profile home schooling advocate and author of books on this and related subjects, until his passing) felt this way about institutional schools' socialization: "If there were no other reason for wanting to keep kids out of school, the social life would be reason enough . . . the social life of the children is mean-spirited, competitive, exclusive, status-seeking, snobbish . . . classes soon divide up into leaders . . . followers, and other outsiders who are pointedly excluded from these groups."

In referring to older children and peer group pressure, John Holt had this to say, "Children who spend almost all their time in groups of other people their own age, shut out of society's serious work and concerns, with almost no contact with any adults except child-watchers, are going to feel that what 'all the other kids' are doing is the right, the best and the only thing to do."

Raymond Moore (along with his wife, Dorothy; other high-profile home schooling advocates and authors on this and related subjects) has also shared much wisdom, such as, "We later became convinced that little children are not only better taught at home than at school, but also better socialized by parental example and sharing than by other little children. This idea was fed by many researchers from Tufts, Cornell, Stanford and California . . . children who spend less of their elective time with their parents than their peers tend to become peer-dependent . . . this tendency has in recent years moved down to preschool, which in our opinion should be avoided whenever good parenting is possible. Contrary to common beliefs, little children are not best socialized by other kids; the more persons around them, the fewer meaningful contacts. We found that socialization is not neutral. It tends to be either positive or negative."

In *Home Style Teaching*, the Moore's define the difference between positive and negative sociability, "*Positive sociability* is the sum of mutual trust, cooperation, kindness, social responsibility, and altruism—best expressed by the Golden Rule's concern for others. *Negative sociability* involves ridicule, rivalry, antagonism, alienation, and narcissism—the 'me first' attitude so prevalent today. . . . "

The *socialization* issue has become the greatest point of contention for those against home schooling. Those with the power to do so have made the institutional school the *societal training ground*, and these impowered people intend to form, shape, and mold the minds of the young to that which is state-serving. State-serving legislation is often *sameness* legislation.

Sameness legislation is not good for the individual, who thrives through uniqueness.

Those who push for school uniforms, with the well-intentioned beliefs that sameness attire will bring equality, push for that which will discourage individuality. Sameness is not equality. All such attempts at bringing equality to children and youth kills individuality, creativity, and uniqueness.

Making children blindly obey those in authority over them suppresses their individual will. To suppress the will in a child is to make a follower, a sheep, and a social weakling. The will of a child should only be guided and directed; that the eventual adult may choose his or her own direction; that he or she may be a leader, a shepherd, and a socially strong person. The unique individual has been a dying breed because of the zombie-like production lines, otherwise known as the institutional schools.

Those children who are home schooled from a young age almost exclusively exhibit greater maturation and wisdom than their same-aged peers. Contrary to popular suspicion, home schooled kids are not introverted nor socially inept. As a rule, these children are outgoing and socially at ease.

8) Aren't home schooled kids confined to their homes?

By the families who home school, it is often called home-based education or life learning. Many home schooling families are very active in and around their communities, as well as in and around their homes. Most home schooling families have a mixture of home, societal and institutional education, both practical and theoretical.

Some home schooling families wonder why the home has such a bad name, having been the backbone of our society and a springboard to multitudes of successful lives in the past. The home is the basic unit of society: to build the home is to build the society; to destroy the home is to destroy the society. Home schooling builds homes. Home schooling builds societies.

Even the home schooling families who are not as active outside of their homes would contend that children who are somewhat confined to a loving, nurturing, safe, home environment are far better off than those children who are confined within an institution that is more often apathetic, usually stifling and sometimes even dangerous. Healthy, happy children would prefer to be confined to the comfortable home of their own family than to be confined to a cold, hard desk, in a four-walled room, in an institution.

Home schooling parents have often found a marked improvement in the health of their children after removing them from institutional school. Particularly the anxiety-based ailments and illnesses (such as stomach disorders, ulcers, headaches, and bed-wetting) seem to disappear.

The great majority of children are simply unable to fully cope with the unnatural environment of the school, just as caged animals do not always easily cope with such unnatural confinement.

Behavioral improvements in children who begin home schooling are usually even more pronounced than health improvements. Stuttering, disobedience, hyperactivity, depression, aggressiveness, passivity, and other difficulties are problems that dissipate when institutional school's out.

Animals in a zoo do not behave as animals living freely. Cage any wild or free animal and observe. Cage your family pet and watch. Send a previously free child to institutional school and look with an honest heart. Children in institutional schools do not behave as children learning freely.

Tragic is the fact that increasing numbers of children are being given Ritalin, Dexedrine, Cylert, Tofranil and other similar drugs under the guise of treating hyperactivity. Some children have even been given drugs without the permission of their parents. There are serious side effects that accompany these drugs.

There is no better medicine available for the general ills of all children than TLC (tender loving care), administered by loving, caring parents. *Iatrogenic diseases* are doctor-caused diseases. There should be such a word for application in cases of *institutional school-caused diseases and disorders.*

There is no better medicine available for the general ills of society than happy, solid homes and families. A secure home environment is a place of refuge to its inhabitants. A happy home is a place of healing, and when children are home schooled there is less to heal from.

The great majority of home schooling families develop a strong bond of friendship and trust. The family home is a place where best friends and best times are to be found. There is no yearning to escape, because they don't feel *imprisoned;* they feel *free* to love and be loved.

9) If home schooled children are protected from the real world by their parents, will they be able to cope as adults?

Many home schooling parents believe that if children are carefully nurtured and protected they will have a healthy foundation to build upon as they grow into adulthood. Children are born full of *intelligence,* but *wisdom* must be learned and acquired a little at a time.

Just as young seedlings grow under the protection of the mature trees in the forest, children must grow under the protection and guidance of their parents in this world. Eventually, the seedlings reach a height where they are subjected to the extremes of the sun, wind, and rain, and their strength is sufficient to withstand the exposure. With proper provision and protection from their parents, children will grow up to be equal to the challenges that will face them.

When left open to the tortures that nature inflicts upon them, young seedlings often wither and die. Children left unprotected or unprovided for, whether it be physical, emotional, social, intellectual, or spiritual provisions, will suffer damage that may not be easily recognized and is not easily repaired.

An adult with a secure, strong sense of self-worth is an adult who was favored with a secure, safe childhood. A strong foundation of character built in childhood is a foundation that will not easily crumble in the teen years nor in adulthood.

One study showed that the Marines that stood up under pressure were the ones who had a favored childhood. There is a popular saying; "Baby the baby and you won't have to baby the man." Children who are forced into *growing up* too fast are less likely to be self-assured, confident, creative, warm, and loving.

Some home schooling parents believe that their children, as teens and adults, tall and strong in wisdom and self-assurance, will be more likely to stand up against the unacceptable in the real world and make it a better world.

It is felt by many home schooling parents that the institutional school does not fulfill the need in children to be taught wisdom. As Ezra Taft Benson has said, "Wisdom is the proper application of true knowledge."

These parents feel that their children need parental influence in order that they may develop wisdom.

By teaching their children all that they have learned, from their own parents and through experience, these parents feel that they will give the best start possible to their children. If life is compared to climbing a mountain, many parents would like their children to pick up the trek where they left off, giving them the highest starting point towards adult life rather than starting at the bottom. Relative to this, Baron Gottfield Wilhelm von Zeibnitz said, "If I appear to see further than others, it is because I sit on the shoulders of giants." These parents try to be the giants, on whose shoulders their children can sit for the furthest view.

The energy of the young must be tempered with good judgment, and these parents feel that they are best suited to teach this to their own children. Victor Hugo said, "One sees a flame in the eyes of the young, but in the eyes of the old, one sees light."

In preparing their children for the real world, many home schooling parents do their best to give their children as favored a childhood as possible. They believe that this effort will not be wasted, as the result will be wise, self-mastered adults. To be a slave to one's mind is foolish; to master one's mind is wisdom. Rather than allowing kids to become fools who follow every fad and fashion, careful parental guidance produces the kind of adults the real world needs.

10) Can home schooled students advance academically in their education?

Home schoolers have found a variety of ways and means to advance in their educations quite easily, since they tend to lead academically.

Many home schooled children work towards and receive high school diplomas and then can proceed to college or university, if they choose to do so.

Even those children who grow to adulthood, completely independent of the public school system, can *challenge* the high school diploma examinations. If they should fail this exam (because of lack of knowledge in the subject matter tested), by taking a few condensed courses they can achieve their high school diplomas in a matter of months.

A number of colleges and universities are quite intrigued by these unique students and will make exceptions to accommodate them. Many home schooled students who have not bothered attaining their high school diploma have passed university entrance exams and usually with flying colors. It is becoming the *rule* rather than the *exception* for a home schooled student to take the top academically.

Although most home schoolers believe in the importance of *a good education,* they recognize that years of schooling will not necessarily command financial or other success.

Charles Franklin Kettering once said that, "The difference between intelligence and an education is this—that intelligence will make you a good living." This statement can help to explain why there are some people walking around with degrees of one kind or another who cannot make the money they need while other people who have very little formal schooling seem to be able to do well.

William Hazlitt wrote, "It is better to be able to neither read nor write than to be able to do nothing else." Although the ability to read and write are vital to secure complete freedom, there are many other elements to the gaining of freedom and success. There are also many elements to intelligence and a *real, practical* education.

There are many success stories of home schooled kids who have reached to academic greatness. It is surprisingly common for these young people to reach levels of genius academically. Some home schooling advocates believe that the occurrence of genius has been squashed due to the institutional schooling experience.

One intense and exhaustive study (the *Smithsonian Report on Genius*) demonstrated that there are essentially three elements necessary for encouraging the occurrence of genius. They are: *quality and quantity time with parents* who are loving and caring, and other such adults; *general isolation from children,* and most especially those peers outside of the family influence; and *generous amounts of free time* allowed for fantasy, play, and exploration within parental guidance.

Harold G. McCurdy, the study director concluded, "The mass education of our public school system is, in its way, a vast experiment on reducing . . . all three factors to a minimum: accordingly, it should tend to suppress the occurrence of genius." These factors are practically guaranteed to be present in an average home schooling home. Home schools should tend to *encourage* the occurrence of genius.

Just a *few* examples of home schoolers who achieved in academic areas of discipline are Alexander Graham Bell, Thomas Edison, Hans Christian Andersen, Agatha Christie, Charles Dickens, C. S. Lewis, George Bernard Shaw, and Albert Schweitzer.

11) **Do home schooled students reach success in other areas, such as the arts, athletics, and the world of business?**

By home schooling, these unique students acquire a strong sense of self-worth, and when coupled with the self-motivation that they learn and retain, they are armed with important ingredients for success, whether it be in academics, the arts, sports or in the world of business. In fact, many home schooling children have excelled in *other* areas.

Many home schooled students have learned to really focus concentration in a selected interest area of their choice, which often results in great achievements. There is often great activity in areas other than academic studies in home schooling families. These *students* are involved in family projects in the arts, in sports, and in entrepreneurial business ventures. Older *students* can be found working with great determination and vigor on their own individual ventures.

It is not unusual for geniuses to crop up in the home schooling crowd—geniuses in academics, geniuses in the arts, geniuses in athletics, and entrepreneurial geniuses. It is becoming the *rule* rather than the *exception* for a home schooled student to take the lead in every area.

Many people who have reached great success were home schoolers. From the past to the present there are many examples of home schoolers achieving greatness.

Some *noted* home schoolers who have achieved in other areas of discipline are Orville and Wilbur Wright, Claude Monet, Leonardo da Vinci, John Quincy Adams, Abraham Lincoln, Franklin Delano Roosevelt, George Washington, Woodrow Wilson, Winston Churchill, Benjamin Franklin, Charles Chaplin, Andrew Carnegie, George Rogers Clark, John Burroughs, and Noel Coward.

12) **What about computers? Won't home schooled kids miss out on new technologies, unless their parents are rich?**

It is true that not all home schooling families can afford to take advantage of new technologies, such as computers, because of a lack of funds. It is also true that although many institutional schools have computers in their premises, this does not guarantee that each individual child will be able to make use of them.

Many home schooled students, armed with eager curiosity and persistence, have found ways and means to reach the *new technological* ends. The benefits of *good old* home schooling are greatly enhanced when coupled with the *new technologies* of this era. The *new technologies* of this era are also greatly enhanced when coupled with the benefits of *good old* home schooling.

Many home schooling kids find ways to take advantage of computers, whether or not they have frequent easy access to them. Some of these kids beg, borrow, and barter for time on computers.

As the price tags of personal computers go down, more home schooling families will be able to purchase them. Perhaps the institutional school system will do more to allow home schooling families access to their publicly funded computers.

13) Do home schooling parents spend five hours a day, five days a week teaching their children?

Most home schooling parents devote very little time to actual teaching, since this is not necessary for children to learn. Surprising to many, it is easily possible for children to keep *up* academically, with their age group, with only *one to three hours* of tutoring per *week*.

Since institutional school teachers spend the majority of their time *disciplining* in their classrooms, they spend much less time actually *teaching* than is assumed by the general public.

Even the teaching time of the teacher cannot be used as an accurate measurement of how much the children have learned. When the class is being *taught* by the teacher, the *minds* of the children are often wandering. Children in institutional schools get *bored*. The *larger* the classroom of students, the *more difficult* it becomes to keep the individual attention of each child.

Since there is little individual attention being paid to each child in the institutional school setting, parents need not spend a great deal of time teaching in order to keep their children up. The average child will receive from *one to three personal responses a day* in the institutional school classroom. The quiet child receives less and the rambunctious child receives more, although negative, responses.

In the home setting, the average child will receive from *one hundred to three hundred personal responses daily* (as found through studies done by Hewitt Research). The questions of the child can be more thoroughly answered. Guidance can more effectively be given. A home schooled child is far more likely to feel important because of the numerous personal responses from a loving parent.

Many home schooling parents read frequently to their young children, as a personal introduction to the written language. Older children in the family are often expected to read to the younger ones. As a poet once penned:

> You may have baskets of wealth untold,
> Coppers of jewels and caskets of gold,
> But richer than I you can never be,
> For I had a mother who read to me.

Although in some home schooling homes the mother is chief teacher of and reader to the children, most home schooling families distribute the teaching and reading more evenly amongst mother, father, and older siblings.

By helping with the education of the younger children, the older children benefit greatly for numerous reasons. They come to understand more fully that which they share with or teach to their siblings. By reading to their younger brothers and sisters, they develop greater oral reading skills. As fellow teachers, guides, and nurturers to their younger siblings, they feel a sense of being needed and necessary to the family.

Most home schooling parents have a positive attitude towards their children's learning abilities. They would agree with Thomas Drier, who said, "One thing that scientists have discovered is that often-praised children become more intelligent than often-blamed ones. There's a creative element in praise."

An integral part of the *teaching* of their children is the time spent working together. Letting children know that they are needed gives them the desire and dedication to utilize innovative ideas in an extended and effort-filled way. Kids need to know they are needed for real reasons, and when they know their parents need their help, they think up ways to help that can be extraordinarily inventive.

Necessity is the mother of invention. Necessity has *several* children. Not only is she the mother of *invention* but of *creativity* and *endurance.* When children sense a real need for their help they will work hard, long, creative, and inventive hours.

The time most home schooling parents spend with their children in real life situations could be termed *practical teaching* or *life learning.* A great deal can be learned without covering *theoretical* lessons. Learning through *experience* is a faster process than learning through *theory.* Someone has said: "I hear and I forget, I see and I remember, I do and I understand." To *understand* is to *learn,* more completely.

"Everyone is a student and a teacher and the world is the classroom" is a phrase coined by Reed A. Benson, which typifies the prevalent home schooling attitude towards learning. Parents in these families believe that little instruction time is necessary for teaching and learning to take place.

Countless hours of instruction have been wasted in institutional schools in the name of learning. Who can measure the time, opportunities, and possibilities lost to children as they sit uncomfortably in their desks, bored *to death*, as they are being taught. What have they learned compared to what they could have learned?

14) Can uncertified teachers teach?

Many teachers and professors would lose their teaching jobs if other than *certified* teachers couldn't teach. Many teachers in the elitist of private schools, some in public, and the majority of instructors in technical schools are not *certified* teachers. University professors are often not trained as teachers.

There are a number of ways to teach, and certified teachers do not have an exclusive market in this area. In reference to paid teachers, it has been penned, "Those who can't do, teach." But do the students of certified teachers learn? The teaching has only been effective if the student has learned. Some studies indicate that, in actuality, an uncertified teacher is more likely to be an effective teacher than one who has been trained and certified to teach.

Teachers are cornered into concentrating on things other than teaching and helping their students learn. Donn Reed (a home schooling advocate, father, and author) has stated, "Teachers today are rated more for their accuracy and punctuality in keeping attendance records than for their achievements in providing an environment in which students can learn."

Anyone who can share their abilities and discoveries in a sincere, enthusiastic way can teach, and the students want to get in on the excitement. A truly good teacher is a *guide* to the student rather than a *master*. When the student desires assistance, it is *given* but never *forced*. If necessary, *persuasion*, which is truly a nobler power than *coercion*, is exercised.

The greatest way to teach is by example, and one who does something well is a teacher just by doing that thing, if others are allowed to observe or assist. To be an example is to teach. To be copied is to teach.

Apprenticeship is a powerful teaching method and has been proven effective for thousands of years. To be taught theory is a chore and difficult work. To *learn through doing* is a natural part of life and human beings were born with the ability to do so.

Many parents who home school their children work together with them. These parents are *mentors*. Their children are *apprentices*. This apprenticeship program embodies the highest form of teaching and learning.

In reference to his own children, Donn Reed wrote, "They learn the most when we stop trying to teach; when we explore and investigate together. We may even have the good fortune to become a little more like them. . . . "

As Reed A. Benson has said, "The ability to care counts more than the ability to teach," and many home schoolers believe this to be true. Who is more likely to really care about a child than his or her own parents? Who has more to loose if a child fails—his parents or a certified institutional school teacher? (See John Holt's *Teach Your Own,* books by Raymond and Dorothy Moore, Glenn Doman, and other books about *domestic education* for more detailed information about uncertified teachers' ability to teach.)

15) Doesn't a child have to be taught to learn?

There is great evidence that shows that the best way to learn is not by being taught but by teaching oneself. Very young children manage to teach themselves to walk and talk, and some even to read and write, before they enter an institutional school. These skills are not easily mastered, and yet without formal instruction these little tiny people do so extremely well. To copy is to learn.

There are many adults in our world's history who have gone through and beyond childhood without entering any institutional school program and have not only been successful but many have been labeled geniuses. They learned to teach themselves, as little children do, and then they continued learning to learn, as most children these days don't—because in institutional schooling, children are taught to sit and be taught. To copy is to learn.

It is a fallacy that children have a short attention span. Even very young children possess the ability to *study* for extended lengths of time when they are interested in something. The key word here is *interest*, as it is next to impossible to get a child to concentrate on something they have no interest in.

Chauncey G. Suites has said that, "Children share with geniuses, an open, enquiring, uninhibited quality of mind." There are studies that have demonstrated that there would be more geniuses if more natural learning was encouraged, rather than institutional school instruction.

On *Wonderstruck*, a CBC children's television show, Bob McDonald has said, "Curious people ask interesting questions." Children, by nature, are extremely curious and ask very interesting questions. Curiosity is a sign of intelligence, and to squelch that curiosity is to squelch intelligence.

When children must endure long hours of instruction, their natural learning *muscles* become listless and their curiosity is weakened. If, on the other hand, children are allowed to learn what they are interested in *at their own pace*, their *learning muscles* and *natural curiosity* flourish.

Creative *muscles* are also at risk of becoming listless or being lost to children because of the institutional school system. John T. Molley said, "Creative people are intellectual detectives . . . the search for truth dominates their lives." This applies to all normal children who have been allowed to grow naturally.

How can children *dominate* their lives with the search for truth or do any *intellectual detecting* from a desk in an institutional school? *Creative* children become *uncreative* adults, *through* and *because* of the institutional school.

How many things have been *learned* without teaching having been *imposed?* Great learning has taken place in many people without the *aid* of instruction. Many of the great inventors and geniuses tended to *resist* being taught and yet were able to learn that which had been previously unthought of.

In reference to real learning, Victor F. Weisskopf has said, "Science is curiosity, discovering things, and asking why, why is it so? . . . We must always begin by asking questions and not by giving answers . . . knowledge has to be sucked into the brain, not pushed into the brain. . . . Avoid, as much as possible, frontal learning: teacher talking, students listening." The institutional schooling authorities continue to insist that teachers try to *push* knowledge into the brains of the children in their charge.

Unfortunately, for the vast majority of children in institutional schools the environment for true learning is not provided. As Ivan Illich has said, "We have come to realize that for most men the right to learn is curtailed by the obligation to attend school." Most caring parents assume that the obligation to attend school brings the reward of learning that would not otherwise be achieved. Every child has a right to learn, but, ironically, this *right is thwarted* by the very institution that was supposedly set up to *afford this right* to every child.

Many educational reform and home schooling advocates hope that institutional schools will eventually provide educational opportunity that equals the average home schooling situation. Educational environments in institutional schools should foster the kind of real learning that is available to almost all home schooling children and should be available to those children who are not fortunate enough to take advantage of the home schooling alternative.

Real learning is whole learning. Home schooling families and other enlightened educators have been taking part in a *whole learning* (also called *holistic learning*) revolution. The rule in the institutional school has been *fragmented bit teaching,* which does not promote true learning. Real learning occurs constantly and continually as an integral part of life: watching, copying, questioning, and searching.

The general educational methods of institutional schools are based upon unnatural laboratory testing of how animals and humans learn nonsensical facts. How nonsensical facts are learned have little or no relation to how sensical information is learned. Frank Smith discusses at length this tragedy in his excellent book, *Insult to Intelligence.*

Institutional schools' standardized systematic instruction of fragmented subjects is an unsuccessful attempt at offering young people a chance to learn and, in fact, deprograms their natural learning abilities. Kids *forget* how to learn when they are not allowed to learn *freely.*

Children are almost guaranteed the opportunity to learn when they are allowed just to live and learn *naturally;* to play, to work, to interact as a part of an intimate group of other people who care about them.

16) What about rote memorization? Isn't it an important learning method?

Rote memorization is a common *teaching* method used in the institutional schools today. Studies are demonstrating this method's ill effects upon the children, who are compelled by their teachers to memorize fact after fact, formula after formula, date after date, name after name, and so forth. The *bright* students *remember* long enough to do well on the exams and the *slow* students don't, but they *all forget* most of what they have memorized, eventually.

Practiced to perfection in Japanese schools, one Japanese professor there claims that rote memorization suppresses true intelligence and inquisitiveness. By the time these students finish their pre-University schooling, not only is their desire to learn squelched entirely, but their self-esteem is battered if not destroyed. Teen suicide is high in Japan.

Most students who are *smart* enough to get into the Japanese universities spend their four years of university *partying!* No longer *forced* into competitive memorizing, *burned out* from years of intense studying, these top-of-the-top, cream-of-the-cream students are *bored* of learning and would rather goof off, get drunk or mess around.

Institutionally imprisoned animals, in zoos and circuses, can be trained to memorize and perform tricks that will bring the applause of an audience. However, animals in the wild, free to learn naturally and instinctively, attain greater levels of true intelligence.

Knowing *how* to learn, how to *reason creatively*, and how to *find* the facts and the answers is far more advantageous than knowing how to memorize facts in bulk. Albert Einstein didn't know his own phone number and wasn't ashamed to say so. He didn't want to *clutter* his mind with *facts* that he could *easily find*.

Children do not learn to *think* by memorizing. Their knowledge and intelligence is increased by following their own questions and following the examples of their mentors, just as they did in order to learn to walk and talk. To copy is to learn.

17) Do home schoolers follow a curriculum similar to the institutional school in their area?

Although most institutional schools try to encourage or enforce compliance to *their* curriculum, many home schoolers do their best to find and follow the curriculum of their choice.

Oliver Wendell Holms stated, "We need education in the obvious more than we need investigation of the obscure." Many parents and educators alike believe that there needs to be a major step back in curriculums. A returning to the teaching of the basics rather than the teaching of theories and opinions.

The opposing camps of so many issues fight for the inclusion of their *side of the story* in the curriculums. The anti-religionists take the religion out of the curriculums and insert their religion: anti-religion, in its place. As the evolutionists removed creation from curriculums, the creationists would remove evolution from the curriculum in order to establish, instead, their theory of creation.

An encyclopedic book series could be created if one were to examine all the differing opinions of all the *experts* and *educators* regarding what should be in the curriculum and what should not.

This complex problem has lead many to feel that only those basic things that are easily agreed upon should be a part of the curriculum. Even still, there are many parents who have particular opinions about how and what their children should be learning in their schooling.

Many parents, educators, and experts are concerned about the lack of morality instruction in the institutional schools. By *removing morality* from curriculums, the kids are learning *immorality*. There is no neutral morality, only morality or immorality. Although there are many who are beginning to agree that it was a mistake to remove *moral* teachings from curriculums, who will agree on what is moral and what is immoral? As an attempt to teach kids *about* right and wrong but not what *is* right and wrong, a new morality called *values clarification* has been conjured up. Teachers encourage children to decide for themselves what is right and wrong; isn't that what kids have been doing since morality was removed from curriculums?

Many will say that it is the parents who should teach their own children their own values of what is right and wrong, or the family morality. How easily is this accomplished when the parents are separated from their children the majority of the time. Home schooling parents feel that quantity time is crucial for instilling values in their children. A little bit of quality time will not erase what has been learned in the majority of a day's learning.

A great many people are bothered by the way our children and we have been taught theories as facts and ideas as eternal truths. Joseph K. Kaplowe, M.D., said that, "When a laboratory can produce the petals of a rose, science will deserve the right to assume the superior attitude prevailing today . . . scientific research must be subservient to Natural Law."

Even scientific *knowledge* can be eventually challenged and proven wrong. Thomas Edison said, "Until man duplicates a blade of grass, Nature can laugh at his so-called scientific knowledge."

More often than not, as the debate wages on, those involved become lost in the middle of their complex issues. Perhaps they need the simple wisdom of Richard Feynman, "The laws of Nature are so simple, we have to rise above the complexity of scientific thought to see them."

We need to make science our *servant* and not our *master*. Edward A. Taub, M.D., F.A.A.P., has explained, "Science is only the human mind's attempt to explain natural laws."

Some parents—those who send their children to institutional school and those who keep their children home—fight a difficult war as they try to bring the curriculum of their children to where it has some semblance of their beliefs. Not everyone is willing to exert the energy necessary to fight in such a seemingly lost cause.

In order to adhere to a curriculum which is compatible with their beliefs, many home schoolers feel forced to *go underground,* or *into the closet,* by the institutional school system in their area.

18) Is there more than one educational method used in home schools?

There are as many ways to home school as there are families doing it. Home schooling is a very diversified method of education which can be molded to suit the needs of the children and family involved.

Families who choose to home school can select between a great number of options, using to a greater or lesser degree any of the following resources and methods: classes and activities within institutional schools; available correspondence courses, private or otherwise; assorted classes, courses, books and manuals; community classes, athletics and activities; museums, art galleries, and other cultural institutions; private or semi-private tutoring; ever-increasing computer learning software; quality radio and television programming; and the vast wealth of knowledge available in the books and audio/visual materials in libraries.

Although some home schoolers toss their television sets when they first turn their homes into centers of learning, quality television pro-gramming is incorporated into the curriculums of most home schoolers. However, the majority of these home schooling parents believe that caution should be exercised when allowing children to watch TV. Not only should the quality of the shows be considered, but the quantity of time spent in front of the tube should be minimal in comparison to other activities and pursuits.

When beginning home schooling, many families use a formal, struc-tured, classroom-like method. These families usually find that their children do not learn well this way, and formal structure gradually gives way to a more natural informal setting, which is much more conducive to learning.

A great many of the home schooling children pursue in the direction that their inquisitiveness propels them. Their parents, who are equipped with a firsthand knowledge of each particular child's particular needs, lovingly guide and encourage them. This renewed *natural* learning or *self-directed* learning approach (*whole* or *holistic* learning), considered by many as a new method, is receiving recent attention and acclaim.

19) What is the *self-directed learning* approach, and does it really work?

Often utilized by home schooling families, this teaching method involves mainly the student. These students study independently, seeking help and guidance as they see fit. They request resources and sources of information when needed. They learn within their own natural schedule rather than *cover* the material put in front of them by an educational *authority*.

Parents of these kids tend to *set a banquet table of resources* before them instead of the standard *spoon* or *force-feed* method common to an institutional school.

By researching on their own in accordance with their own interests, they learn to *reason and think* rather than to *remember and forget.* Unlike institutionally schooled students, home schooled students tend to continue to be inquisitive. These students search for answers to their questions. Genius is born of inquisitiveness. As Albert Einstein once said, "I have no particular talent, I am merely extremely inquisitive." As many other geniuses have, Albert Einstein did poorly in his institutional schooling.

Because, as Jean Renoir said, "Learning is being able to see the relationship between things"; children need time to recognize these relationships in a natural way. They need time to learn, naturally.

One home schooling mother said, "Children do not learn on schedule, it is completely alien to their nature," and many parents agree. Just as you can lead a horse to water but you can't make him (or her) drink, you can instruct an individual but you can't make him (or her) learn.

Left to learn according to nature's design, most children will play a great deal until they reach twelve years of age, at which time their *biological clock* or *program* says that they are ready for fine-tuned academic learning.

Relatively few children in the last one hundred or so years have been allowed to learn according to nature's design. Those who have are the ones who easily learn in a short time what their *institutional schooling peers* tried to learn in six or more years of study.

Children who haven't learned to read until age twelve are not left behind in the intellectual dust of their schooling peers; rather, they seem to soar past in a very short time due to what could be termed the *catch-up phenomenon.* It is normal and natural for children to resist academic learning until puberty, at which time they will catch up and pass their institutional schooling peers.

Onlookers of some home schools might wonder how and what the children are learning, because the kids seem to spend so much time *playing.* Besides the fact that it takes very little *academic study* time to keep up with institutional school peers, there is very real value in play.

The ability to play is a sign of intelligence. To play is to experiment, to practice, to act, to sing, to dance, to exercise, to read, to write, to calculate, to create, and to learn naturally. When children play, a great deal of learning happens that may be incalculable, but learning happens.

Children should be allowed to play. Even older kids need to play, as a part of natural learning and discovery. Many an adult would benefit from playing as children do.

Numerous great inventions have been brought to this world through and because of the *playing* with ideas. Inventors *play* with ideas. Scientists *play* as they experiment. Composers *play* with tunes. Writers *play* with words.

Through play is often born laughter. Not only is laughter the *best medicine,* but the ability to laugh and make others laugh is also a sign of intelligence. A good sense of humor is good for the mind and body. Parents should appreciate a good sense of humor in their children.

Unfortunately, the institutional school at large suppresses natural learning, play, and laughter. Militaristic control in the schools removes freedom of expression in children. Kids are forced into conforming, thereby losing much of their uniqueness, creativity, and individuality.

There is little that is natural about a large number of children of the same age being kept in uncomfortable desks, *locked up* with an adult *stranger,* in a room for five to six hours a day, five days a week, nine to ten months a year, for twelve years more or less.

Among the numberless words of wisdom of John Holt are these, "It is not that I feel that school is a good idea gone wrong, but a wrong idea from the word go. It's a nutty notion that we can have a place where nothing but learning happens, cut off from the rest of life."

Even adults can learn many new things, who according to many experts are past the optimum age for great strides in learning. Old adults can learn new tricks, particularly when a natural learning method is utilized. Adults can learn new languages. Previously illiterate adults can learn to read and to write.

By following a self-directed learning approach and with the aid of a cooperative guide, adults can learn as children and babies so easily do. In a relatively short period of time, illiterate adults have become literate. The learner asks the guide what a particular word looks like and the guide writes the word. As illiterate adults ask their guides to write the words that they are curious about, their reading vocabulary grows in accordance with their interest. Eventually, the learner begins to recognize *rules* of the language and can then begin to figure out new words for themselves.

When the institutional schools begin to encourage the self-directed learning approach, the illiteracy problem that is running rampant today will begin to fade. Many other educational failures will also be cured when this return to nature in education and learning is accomplished.

20) Are home schooled children tested, and if so, how often?

Some home schooled children are tested and the frequency of examinations depends on what is agreed upon by the authorities and parents involved. Most home schooling parents, however, disagree that testing has merit.

Parents who home school their children independent of the state (provincial) schooling system rarely use testing as part of their educational program. They believe that testing is an inferior form of evaluation and is usually counterproductive.

Testing does not help learning. Outwardly imposed testing is not a positive tool to the tested child or person. To be tested usually brings tension. A bad testing method is known by its discouraging influence on the learner. Testing methods of the institutional schools are usually, if not always bad.

A good testing method is known by its encouraging influence on the learner. Self-testing can be helpful to the learner, and many children have their own methods of measuring themselves through their own types of testing. Children rarely, if ever, impose bad testing methods upon themselves.

Tests are more often than not inferior at assessing true intelligence or learning. Most tests of the institutional school are based upon *fractional bit* learning and not upon whole learning, which is what most home schoolers are interested in.

When home schooled children are tested by institutional school teachers and authorities, their whole learning and true intelligence is not *tapped*, because the institutional school tests are not geared to find such knowledge. Institutional tests are designed to find the *bits* of information that the institutional school curriculum has provided or imposed.

The vast majority of home schooling parents believe that tests in schools are used as aids to teachers who simply cannot monitor the progress of numerous students. Home schooling parents need no such aids for monitoring their children. The progress of their children is far more easily seen, given the closeness of the relationship and schooling situation.

People, young or old, are not machines that can be easily monitored. The human brain is monumentally more complex than a computer, and monumentally more than mankind can comprehend. The ability of a test to be able to measure knowledge and intelligence in an individual is being questioned more and more by clear thinking people. Even the ubiquitous *IQ test* is being questioned more and more by *authorities* in varying relative fields of study.

Testing is an aid to teachers in grouping, labeling and categorizing students. Perhaps because funding per *learning disabled* child is greater in dollars than for *normal* children, more learning disabled children seem to crop up. By the same token, funding per *gifted* child is greater and many more children are being labeled gifted by institutional schools.

Unfortunately, students are often held back or even pushed ahead by an arbitrarily placed label, which was based upon one or just a few tests. One failed test can indeed fail one lifetime.

21) If a child is doing poorly in home school, isn't it the parents' fault and shouldn't the child be placed into institutional school?

When a child fails in an institutional school, that child is usually blamed for the failure, not the teacher, nor the system of education. Many home schooling parents believe that if a child is doing poorly in one or more areas, that with patience and encouragement they will improve, and numerous cases have shown that they do.

Among home schooled children, who appear to show little or even no advances, there occurs the *catch-up phenomenon.* Studies have indicated that children often *wait* until about the age of twelve to *catch up* with their peers, particularly in academic areas. Theorists conclude, in reference to this *phenomenon,* that the child's ability to learn academically does not usually fully come together until the approximate age of twelve years.

Few people expect parents to remove their children from an institutional school, even after countless failures. Many children are failing all the way through thirteen years of standard schooling, and this seems acceptable. Yet, even after only a period of months of home schooling, critics of this method expect only success.

The younger the child is when transferring from institutional school to home school, the more easily the transition is made and the greater the success that is realized. For children who have never been institutionalized in a school, there is no need for a transition. There is just a natural learning progression. These children learn readily as they always have.

For children who have been institutionalized in a school, there will be a *withdrawal* period, not unlike an actual withdrawal sickness. The length of time that this withdrawal will last depends largely on the length of time the child has been institutionalized in school. These children must overcome their dependency on their *peer group,* the *teachers* and *the school,* their *pseudo-family and home.* They must also remember how to learn or relearn how to teach themselves, rather than simply attempt to memorize that which is *spoon* or *force-fed* to them by their teachers.

Home schooling parents are not generally pitting their children in a race to succeed within any arbitrarily conceived time limit. These parents simply wish to provide the best opportunities for success to their children. Even when advances are slow, success can be realized.

22) If one home schooling situation has failed, is the educational form deemed a failure?

When a child fails in an institutional school, it is not assumed that every child thereafter is destined to fail because one child did. In the institutional schools, however, many children are failing. Even when they *pass* their grades and go on to finish school, they have often failed to learn. There are many facets of learning, and many children, as products of the institutional schools' *assembly lines*, have failed to learn what they should have and could have otherwise learned.

Because of the numerous children who fail and have failed through the institutional schools, there is reason to consider this educational form a failing one. There is so much that institutionally schooled children have not learned by the time they finish school.

After having tried home schooling briefly, some families have decided against it because they felt at the time that it didn't work for them. It is more often the case, though, that the institutional school *supervision*, or *interference*, hampers the learning processes of the home school.

Occasionally, the press grabs hold of a story about one child who has done poorly in a home schooling situation and the myth that this is common, or will occur continually, is perpetuated.

Actual cases of children failing at home schooling are few and far between, and in fact, even children with severe learning disabilities have thrived in a home schooling situation.

What is a case of a *late bloomer* may be misinterpreted as a failing child. More correctly, a *normal bloomer* would be labeled as failing by institutional school systems' standards. Children who resist academic learning before the age of twelve are normal.

There are countless children who are deemed poor learners who are very bright and intelligent. Many people, later proven highly intelligent or even genius, have previously done extremely poor in their institutional schooling. (See John Holt's *Teach Your Own* for insights to learning disabilities.)

Kids who do not easily memorize nonsense may be labeled failing. In trying to perfect the teaching methods to an exacting science, memoriza-

tion of *nonsense* has become a big part of institutional school *learning.*
(See Frank Smith's *Insult to Intelligence.*)

Rather than allowing children to pursue learning on a natural,
progressive, and successive path, institutional schools try without success
to dissect and force-feed fragments of knowledge to *sitting-still* children.
By *feeding* children *fragments* of information, children are expected to
memorize and learn what seems to be nonsense to them.

Learning *nonsense* is very difficult. Learning *naturally* is very easy.
Children don't strain and work at learning to crawl, walk, and talk. It
comes quite easily to them and it is fun. They *enjoy* natural learning.
Kids *don't* enjoy the memorizing of *nonsense facts.* By being *forced* to
learn nonsense, kids *lose* their desire to learn. They lose their intelligence.

What intelligence a baby is naturally endowed with can be repressed
or enhanced. Although the *nature versus nurture* battle still persists, most
of us stand in the middle of that issue, believing a little of both of the
opposing sides. Some of us are born more intelligent than others, some
less. This intelligence can be *beaten* out of us or encouraged to *grow* to
great heights.

Most home schooling parents are trying their best to give their children that which will enhance and encourage intelligence, rather than to
repress or damage it. For this reason, they sometimes feel compelled to
avoid interference from the institutional schooling authorities, by home
schooling *independent of the school system.*

If home schooling children do not conform to the institutional school's
time table as they follow their natural biological clock, they may be
deemed failing and be forced back into the *classroom.* It is difficult for
home schooling families to work successfully with the institutional schools.

23) Won't home schooling children miss out on the advantages of starting institutional schooling early?

It is a common misconception that an early institutional schooling start is a better start. No studies indicate that children who start in an institutional school setting early do better academically because of their early start.

On the contrary, numerous studies indicate that children who start in an institutional school setting later do better academically later because of their late start. Experts have concluded that the best start children can have is from their homes. (See Raymond and Dorothy Moore's *School Can Wait* and *Better Late Than Early;* and Hewitt Research information.)

There are many children who have done no academic schooling before the age of twelve or thirteen and then have gone on to astound onlookers as they exhibit the little-known *catch-up phenomenon* in their academic learning. Puberty, not infancy, is the naturally programmed beginning of the brain's complete academic learning powers.

There is no evidence to suggest that there is any advantage to children in attending institutional school whatsoever. There is conclusive evidence that there is great advantage to children in avoiding institutional school. Home schooling is clearly being proven superior.

The popular theory of this day is that children have a greater ability to learn than adults do. The younger the child, the greater the ability to absorb facts and information. This belief has further propelled proponents of extremely early, mandatory institutional school attendance. These advocates of earlier aged, mandatory institutional school entrance fear that these fertile young minds will be lost if not caught and planted in early and quickly.

The ability to absorb facts is not the only measurement of intelligence. A free animal in the wild possesses greater useful individual intelligence than an imprisoned animal in captivity. The tamed pet may amaze onlookers with delightful tricks that have been learned from a master through various ways and means, but the ability to survive and adapt may be lost. Creative inquisitive thinking has likely been suppressed in the animal.

This ability to absorb facts is also no measurement of readiness for academic learning. Many recent studies indicate that children must develop in a variety of physical ways before they are optimally ready for reading, writing, calculating and other forms of school studying. Children who go to institutional school early will more likely develop myopia (nearsightedness), because they are forced into close-range focusing for extended periods of time. The eyes of a young child are not ready for the intense study that the institutional school demands of them.

Studies have indicated that even adults have great ability to learn. Adults can learn to speak and write new languages, master new arts and athletics, and learn a vast array of new skills. Their fear of trying poses the greatest hindrance to them, not that they are too old to learn. Many experts claim that adults have even greater ability to learn new things, given their longer attention span, more highly developed motor control, greater reasoning powers and earned wisdom.

Although children have great intelligence, this ability is not coupled by great wisdom. Parents have the right to teach and guide their children towards the accumulation of greater wisdom, that the acquired knowledge will be put to proper use.

True, it is, that even infants can learn and absorb *genius-level* amounts of data, like little, cuddly, mobile computers. What is most important is that children (and the importance escalates the younger their age) learn in the atmosphere of their *comfortable family home* rather than the *clinical institutional school.*

On either side and in the midst of the *better baby* theory, home schooling families take residence. Whether these families incorporate flash card sessions and extensive, exhaustive learning episodes, or they just sit back and watch their children learn and grow, like watching lilies in a field, they do what they believe best.

There are those with a *leave them alone and they'll come home* philosophy who are adamantly against *teaching* their children *academic subjects* from infancy. Some feel strongly about cooperating in letting nature take its natural course and don't wish to *pressure* their babies into learning *tricks.*

Parents who swing to the opposing side desire to give their tiny youngsters a gentle boost towards genius. Some are determined to have *better babies.* A few of them frantically go to great lengths to ensure the genius of their children.

The majority of home schooling families, however, live and learn somewhat in the middle of either extreme. By using the knowledge that babies are brilliant, in a moderate and relaxed manner, parents can guide their children as they stop and smell the roses along the path to genius.

Parents who want to give their children a learning advantage can simply provide a banquet table (buffet style) of learning materials, resources, and activities. Rather than only being offered one selected subject of study or activity at any given time, children delight in a smorgasbord of things to do. Even when little is provided, children's inquisitiveness and creativity turns poor opportunity into rich results.

Institutional schools could adopt such natural and free-flowing educational methods and it would be greatly beneficial if they did. But the love and security of the child's home can not be duplicated, only inadequately substituted. As Gandhi once said, "There is no school equal to a decent home and no teacher equal to a virtuous parent."

It is true enough that there are children who's homes are lacking in security and who's parents are lacking in love. Institutional schools and homes can pull up the slack, but the government shouldn't pull kids out of homes where they are safe, secure and properly provided for. There are certain bounds in this area which should not be overstepped, and great caution should be exercised when the government authorities are considering the removal of children from their homes and families, for whatever reason.

The governing body and its institutions could do much to provide assistance to parents and families who want to improve their situations, in whatever area of concern, be it financial, social, emotional, intellectual, or physical. The governing body has done much to frustrate growth and success in families, by stepping in inappropriately. Wisdom must be used in determining what action to follow in each differing circumstance.

(See Raymond and Dorothy Moore's *School Can Wait* and *Better Late Than Early* for more detailed and substantiated information on why children should start school later rather than earlier.)

24) **If institutional schooling isn't advantageous, why, then, have authorities lobbied for mandatory institutional schooling and mandatory early entrance age to institutional schooling, in particular?**

Mandatory institutional schooling has not been brought about for the educational or social advantage of children but to control and maintain a particular order in society.

In the 1870s, in major cities, there were roving street gangs of children: orphans and those children who were left unsupervised by factory-working parents. The authorities made schooling mandatory in order to *get the children off of the streets.*

There are those who claim that institutional schooling is not much more than a *glorified day-care, child watch service,* or even a *teen prison,* where children are taught to conform to that which the *state* has determined is *good* for the *state.*

Institutional schools should have voluntary attendance rather than mandatory attendance. Forcing children to attend an institutional school for ten years is not unlike a *ten-year prison sentence* with evening, weekend and summer passes. What are children guilty of that they should be sentenced to a minimum of ten years in an institution? Why should the government assume that children will benefit more from this artificial and unnatural confinement than they will from being in their natural home and with their family?

Children and their parents should be innocent until proven guilty. Innocent children should be free to live and learn, in and around their homes and communities. Parents should be free to teach their children as they see fit, within reasonable bounds, meaning as long as there is no proven detrimental neglect nor abuse to their children. Freedoms in education have been removed from families and there are those who seek to remove the freedoms of individuals further in this and other areas of living.

While it is proper for the government to provide for those who are not being provided for, it is not proper for the government to usurp parental responsibility and enforce provision where provision is not needed nor wanted. A democratic government should be a government *by the people, for the people;* not *by the government, for the government.*

Home schooling focuses on the needs of the individual child, and by so doing, the needs of the child are more likely met, resulting in a very healthy growing up for that child. Home schooling children are more inclined to learn to do what they feel is *right*, rather than to learn to do whatever they are told or whatever the group is doing.

Institutional schooling is not good for the individual nor the *state* in the long run. Children who grow to become self-assured adults who tend to lead others will do far more good for society than children who have grown to become unsure adults who tend to follow others.

25) How do institutionally schooled children ever become self-assured as adults?

Self-assuredness is born of a healthy self-esteem—something rarely cultivated in the institutional school setting. The isolated instances where kids' self-esteems are fostered are when they are popular and well liked by both teachers and fellow students. It takes a great deal of the *right stuff* to be popular with your peers and teacher's pet at the same time!

Even a child's name can be crucial to not only his or her popularity but to schooling success as well. Some researchers have found that children with names that are popular with teachers do better in school (this has been penned the Pygmalion effect). Unusual names can pose a threat to successes in school. Some names almost ensure bad marks and lesser treatment.

For some young adults, there is much to overcome on the road to self-assuredness. Institutional schools leave scars more often than not. The victims of these *state school systems* are the majority of the students. Few kids escape being damaged.

It takes time to rebuild lost and lowered self-esteem. Nature has generously given a savior: time. Time heals all wounds. The body and soul have an ability to heal itself, but it takes time.

Many adults begin *home schooling, self-schooling* or *de-schooling* after completing formal institutional schooling. Through great perseverance, the *herded-sheep syndrome* can be overcome. These days, average adults don't really fully *grow up* socially, emotionally and even intellectually until their late twenties or early thirties.

In contrast, children in our past became adults in their early teens without any loss of growing up. In actuality, the teen of today tends to accomplish little of value or worth and, therefore, wastes a part of life that could have been time so much more wisely utilized. Time, as well as other commodities, was not wasted in the recent past as it tends to be today.

One major positive element that is so often lacking in the institutional school environment is worthy work and service. Working and serving others is very building to self-esteem. To serve is to love, and to be needed is to feel loved. It is common to begin to learn about giving, as an adult. This knowledge or skill needs to be developed before adulthood, beginning at a very young age and continuing throughout all of one's life. Many home schooling families make working, serving and sharing an integral part of education.

Responsibility is an attribute, closely related to self-assuredness, that is much more effectively taught in homes than in institutional school. To be herded as cattle; to be force-fed information, programs and activities as a group; to be coerced into evaluations and tests; to be criticized and compared to each other, children are not taught to be responsible for themselves as individuals.

Institutional schooling tends to produce unindividuals who often aimlessly follow the masses. Home schooling produces individuals who usually purposefully lead the masses.

26) Won't home schooled children miss out on a normal childhood?

In the 1800s, a normal childhood was completed by the early teens as adulthood began. Adulthood was achieved by the mid-teens. Average fifteen-year-old *boys* or *girls* could completely manage a home, a farm, a ranch, a business, almost equally as well as their parents.

In this century, however, it has become expected and acceptable in our society for teenagers to roam with little or no purpose, to menace society, and to rebel against authority and the establishment.

The first major *counterculture* emerged because of institutionalized schooling and it's *peer-dependence syndrome.* A major counterculture emerges approximately every ten to fifteen years (according to Hewitt Research). Many institutionally schooled students are *burned out, sick and tired,* and *generally rebellious* by the early and even before the teen years. Although considered *twentieth century normal* by many, this is not part of a natural childhood.

Home schooling deletes the generation gap that institutional schooling installed. Home schooled children, after enjoying a natural childhood, have grown into responsible, mature, adult-like teens, as capable as adults in many ways. More often than not, the home schooled attain *average, middle years maturity and wisdom* in their *twenties.* Institutionally schooled children miss out on a natural childhood.

27) Isn't the 9-to-4 daily regimen of school attendance good for children in order to prepare them for the 9-to-5 daily regimen of adult work life?

Twelve or more years of daily 9-to-4 institutional school attendance is not good for children, nor is it necessary to prepare them for the daily 9-to-5 work attendance in adulthood. Just as a good defense is often the best offense, a secure, solid and good foundation in childhood is the best preparation for the work life and challenges of the adult world.

It is unfortunately often the case that numerous institutional schooling authorities, particularly teachers, believe so strongly in the daily 9-to-4 attendance being good for the students, that this becomes crucial to marks and even passing or failing. These teachers believe that attendance is such a major factor that they will actually lower the true marks of the students if there has been any absence. Children have been failed because of poor attendance.

This practice is quite common and the marks of the students don't always reflect their actual performance. Because of poor attendance, students have been failed even when their actual performance has been outstanding. The lowering of the marks is usually unnoticed and unseen because of the unavailability of the teacher/school's records to the parents and students.

Simple attendance, deemed worth more than performance, passes many students from grade to grade. They receive marks for merely being there. In the adult work world, this sad situation is often repeated, as many adults receive a paycheck for just punching in and out each day.

Many argue that the 9-to-5 adult work regimen is the best and most productive work system. It is certainly not the only work system. Others cry for more diversified and individualized work systems that have been successful in the past and which continue to be so. The *9-to-5, punch in/punch out and get paid work system* just may be a *thing of the past* as superior systems become the *wave of the future*.

28) Isn't positive reinforcement, like happy faces, stickers, check marks and good grades, good for children?

Rewards such as happy faces, stickers and so on are far better than punishments like big bad X's, dunce caps and strappings. An outwardly implemented reward system, however, is only a step (although a tall step) above an outwardly implemented punishment system.

Through these reward systems, children learn to perform only when applauded. Children feel this conditional system requires them to continually maintain a certain level of performance in order to merit admiration. This is a type of *conditional love.*

An inward sense of responsibility to themselves as individuals is not cultivated. Self-motivation, self-respect and love of self are lacking. This condition can eventually lead to *syndromes* such as over-competitiveness, over-achievement, neurotic-perfectionism, excess-materialism, on one side, and depression, self-denial, self-hate and suicide, on the other.

Far superior a system is one where the children are loved for who they are and not for what they can do. For these children, acquired skill and knowledge are sufficient rewards in and of themselves. These children perform, not for the applause, but for the fun in performing. They work, not for the reward, but for the satisfaction of working. They give, not for what they will receive, but for the joy in giving.

Children who are educated and nurtured in this unconditional loving way are more apt to love themselves and others unconditionally. These children will grow up and go on to contribute to the people of the world around them, because they care about the people, not the power nor the money that they could conquer.

When Edmund Vance Cooke said, "Perhaps the reward of the spirit who tries, is not the goal but the exercise," he may have been indirectly referring to those who fail or lose the prize. The exercise exerted during learning activity is a reward for the natural learner. Reaching a self-determined *goal* is a final reward in natural learning. Winning an outwardly determined *prize* is insignificant compared to the real rewards of natural learning.

29) Are any institutional schools implementing successful home schooling methods?

In a desperate attempt to solve the many problems faced in institutional schools today, schooling authorities are frantically looking for *new* ideas. Many of these so-called new ideas are simply redressed old ones. Pilot projects that resemble the home school environment somewhat are being implemented.

One such idea is to create the *country school atmosphere* by placing younger through older students in one classroom situation, where the older students help the younger ones. This has proven more effective in enhancing learning than the same-age segregated classrooms but not more effective than a home school.

Another similar idea is to provide a feeling of security and continuity by keeping the teacher and classroom of students together over the twelve to thirteen years of schooling: a *family-type atmosphere* with a *same-parent image*. This *could* be an improvement over the major readjustments made yearly in the average schooling situation but not an improvement over the actual family and parents.

Open classrooms and other more flexible approaches that resemble *the home school experience* have been experimented with by institutional schools. Rigid methods of the *old institutional school* are slowly being seen as archaic by many educators in the public or state school systems.

The ideal schooling is home and family schooling. Where true family institutions are unable to provide for their children, the government institution can provide *home and family-like* institutions for these children to fall back on.

The home school has been labeled by some as a *lab of educational experimenting*. It has also been termed *the classroom of tomorrow*. As home schools continue to *produce* scores of successful students, the surrounding world around will look to them for solutions to educational problems.

30) How much do certified teachers and schooling authorities know about home schooling?

Unfortunately, the majority of teachers and authorities actually know very little if anything about home schooling. Many of these professionals assume knowledge and expertise in an area in which they have no practical experience and perhaps a great deal of misinformation. Some then proceed to critique or advise while knowing so very little about home schooling.

Many institutional teachers and authorities are quick to discount anything positive about home schooling. These narrow-minded individuals are quick to cut down this creatively successful educational alternative. Perhaps when such people fight against those who have found enlightenment we should think of the words of Jonathan Swift: "When a true genius appears in the world you may know him by this sign, that the dunces are all in confederacy against him."

Fortunately, growing numbers of *state* school teachers and supervisors are educating themselves about home schools, usually through close association with home schoolers. These *teachable* teachers and supervisors are also delving into the written sources of information about practical home schooling situations and success stories.

31) Can low income or welfare recipient families home school their children?

Sometimes said by home schoolers, "All you need to successfully home school is *love and a library card.*" There need not be an abundance of money for a child to learn, although money can always bring advantage in all areas of living to those who have it. Families in difficult circumstances have found solutions to problems encountered after deciding to home school. What many home schooling families lack financially is often made up for with ingenuity, hard work and unconventional methods.

There are home schooling *networks* of families in most areas, and there is usually a *help each other* attitude amongst them. Learning exchanges are utilized. Free learning opportunities are taken advantage of.

The greatest barrier to welfare recipients would easily be the interference of well-meaning, but fact-ignorant, welfare workers. Women on welfare are targets for the most intrusion. Some of these welfare families do their best not to share with their workers that they are home schooling.

If a worker became aware of a family's home schooling activities, the parent/s would do well to ask the worker to read a bundle of books before they discuss the matter further.

Hopefully, welfare systems at large will allow more freedoms in educational choices. An individual's lack of opportunity to succeed financially should not be deemed as an inability to succeed in other areas.

A welfare recipient family can home school successfully as long as welfare workers don't intrude by usurping parental authority. A low-income family can home school successfully.

As more welfare workers become educated about the home schooling alternative, they will be better equipped to play a supportive, rather than a counterproductive, role to these families.

32) What about less educated parents?

If children are shown the basics (the three R's)—reading, writing, and arithmetic—they can take that educational foundation and build upon it by pursuing the field of study of their choice.

A great many home schooled students have gone on to specialize and succeed in particular fields of study, even when their parents have been partially or even totally ignorant or uneducated in those fields.

Just as champions in athletics and the arts have often succeeded *in spite of* parents who lack in skills and knowledge particular to these special areas, so, too, have champions in academics succeeded.

Parents need not know all the answers in order to encourage their children to seek after answers to their own questions. Acting as guides, parents can be instrumentally helpful to their children. Parents can direct their children to resource sources and materials.

Simply by cheering their children on, parents can be vitally important sources of encouragement. Parents can give their children the gifts of self-esteem and self-motivation: two key ingredients to the success of an individual.

In order to aid their children in excellence pursuits, it is not necessary for parents to excel in any discipline of study—be it academic, of the arts, or athletics. Parents can help their children achieve a *first-generation* expertise by being *supportive*. They need not play an *instructive* role in the refining and specializing of their children's education.

33) Isn't it almost impossible for a single-parent family to home school?

Although there are obvious barriers to home schooling for a single parent who must work, there are those who have found ways to do it. Some parents in this situation are able to involve their child/ren in their work, at their work place, or at home. Some find other home schoolers who will help. Some older children care for themselves, learn on their own while alone, and home school with their parents after work.

Just as society's trend towards institutionalizing infant and child care precludes a single-parent's options for parenting little children in the home, educational opportunities for school-aged children in the home are also difficult for a single parent to attain. Most of those who believe in home school also believe in *home-centered* infant and child care. This belief embodies the assumption that a *home-centered* upbringing brings stability, security, and a positive sense of self to the individual.

Hopefully, in the future these problems will be alleviated through needed changes in governmental programs. Each family should have more opportunity to personally raise, nurture and teach their own children. If institutional day-care/school was the exception for those who really want or need it and home child-care/school was the rule, individuals, families, homes, communities, cities, countries and the world would be strengthened instead of being broken down to and beyond the sad state that it now is.

34) How do I know if I am capable of home schooling my children?

You are capable of home schooling your child/ren if you can write your name, read this sentence, count your fingers and toes, afford a library card, and if you love your children. This statement will likely appear extremely simplistic, but it is essentially true.

Because you have the ability to read and understand all or part of this book, you obviously have the ability necessary to teach your children at home. Those who have difficulty reading this probably can teach their children at home. Bare-basic literacy is a sufficient qualification in order for parents to give a literacy start to their children. Some less-literate parents have begun the home schooling process for their children and end up taking great learning strides themselves.

Because you are interested in giving your child/ren the advantage of home schooling, you obviously have enough love for your child/ren to guide and nurture them and their growth at home. Every family stands to benefit from this natural learning process, often called home schooling.

There are some people who are quick to recognize the advantages of home schooling but are also quick to doubt their ability to do it themselves. If these self-doubters can get past their fears, they too can successfully home school their children.

If you possess just a little self-confidence, you can successfully school your children at home. A strong sense of self-direction will be helpful if you come up against opposition, which most home schoolers do.

35) I've read a little about home schooling and I'm convinced that it's for me. Now what do I do?

If you are interested in the idea of home schooling but lack confidence in your ability to know what it is all about and what to do: read, read, read . . . about home schooling.

After you have read a number of articles and books on the subject, you may find that you have an overwhelming desire to jump in with both feet and begin home schooling your children. You just know that it is right for you.

You may not be sure which direction to take, since there are so many ways to home school. Try not to let this *lost* feeling overwhelm or discourage you. Look carefully at the options in front of you and try to get a feel for which is more your style. Begin with one approach and transfer to another if you find that what you have chosen does not work for you. You need not get locked in to something that isn't right for you and your family.

There are two *extreme* ends of the home schooling scale and many variations in between. If you find your opinion swaying to one side or the other, remember to respect others' opinions and hope that they will respect your's.

On the conservative side of the scale is the type of home schooling where you work very closely with the schooling authorities by being registered with a particular school, a superintendent, or the correspondence school department. Either way, you answer to the schooling authorities and you have the least freedom in choosing the educational program of your child.

On the more controversial side of the scale is the type of home schooling where you work independent of the schooling authorities. This form of home schooling has been labeled *closet* home schooling by some, but the families implementing this method are far from *in the closet* in their educational methods.

In the midst of the formerly mentioned extremes are the many mixtures of all the options open to you as you survey the home schooling banquet before you. There are a multitude of books, texts, classes, courses, programs, and so forth to choose from.

The home schooling experience is an individual and everchanging one. Just as the parenting experience is unique to each parent because of the personal choices available, home schooling programs are unique to each family due to the possibility of choices. Home schooling books and articles contain ideas and instructions to help you begin your home schooling journey, regardless of the path you choose to follow.

You will find that a carefully formulated *Letter of Intent to Home School* is probably where you should begin, on this alternative education trek. This letter, a foundation letter, can be modified and utilized for many purposes: to family, friends, inquirers, politicians, and, of course, schooling authorities. When writing this crucially important letter, you may wish to keep in mind this five-point plan:

1) Introduce and inform the schooling authority of your decision.
2) Educate the educational official about home schooling in general.
3) Express briefly your reasons for choosing this alternative.
4) Explain your planned curriculum in general terms.
5) Conclude by bowing out gracefully, although firmly.

Remember to exercise strength as you assert your rights. Put your best into this letter. Your intelligence will be judged by the educators who read it. Their decision to cooperate with you or fight against you will be based on how you come across in your letter. Get help in composing it, if you need it. Of all the many things I've ever written, my *Letter of Intent to Home School* was something I worried over the most. Worrying didn't help at all! Once I settled down and just wrote it, I did my best and left it at that. As I grow in wisdom and ability, I improve upon it.

Don't bother delving into your beliefs and philosophies in detail. There is no need to stir up possible controversies. Be prepared, though, to refute any authority's stance that would rob you and your family of freedoms in education. If you receive a militant *no*, you can then dispute particular theories in greater detail. You can utilize quotes, experts' opinions, examples from history, and research findings to defend your stand.

If the schooling authority thinks that you stand firmly on firm ground, he or she won't want to battle with you. The institutional school does not want to take on a fight that *they* just may lose. They look bad enough to the mass populous as it is. There are many independent *high-profile* home schooling families that the institutional schools don't bother *taking on.* Generally, the schools will try to take to court only the families that will look incompetent to the public. Whether or not you decide to make your schooling choice *known,* the *Letter of Intent to Home School* is something you should take the time to do. You may find that you need it some time in the future.

36) How can I create a curriculum that is compatible with our ideals?

There are a great number of alternatives in curriculum available to home schooling families. Some home schooling organizations would direct you to *home schooling* curriculums that you could make use of, covering material that is compatible to your beliefs.

Any curriculum costs you money, though, and many home schooling families feel that it is not worth the worry, trouble, and money spent. Although usually cheaper, most institutional school correspondence curriculums are tedious, boring, and loaded with *filler* material.

The curriculums that allow for the most flexibility are the most worth looking into. A *just-starting* home schooling family may decide that they need to reach outward for a *narrow guide* curriculum to follow because they lack inner confidence. Most home schooling families graduate toward less rigidity in the curriculum that they choose.

Although it is common for beginning home schooling families to feel the need for a *curriculum crutch,* the majority of home schooling families gravitate towards a natural learning approach, where the kids are allowed and even encouraged to *go on their own* in their studies.

The parents of these families act as guides to learning, just as in their roles as guides in parenting in general. They are there to suggest, encourage, council, direct, care, and especially to love.

The transition from ages four/five to ages five/six is only a noticeable one when institutional teachers and schooling is employed. Parents who opt out of *school* and just continue to be parents as they thus far have, watching their children grow, take part of no transition.

Many home schooling parents believe in the natural curriculum: the built-in curiosity of the child. There need not be *planned learning.* Learning will take place, even in less favored circumstances. The way a parent can best facilitate an environment for learning is by providing reasonable freedoms, love, support, and guidance.

37) Is it possible for me to make sure my children are covering all the subjects?

Too much attention has been given to the covering of subjects and not enough attention to real learning, or whole (holistic) learning; which does not happen simply because fragmented material has been covered.

In institutional schools, the so-called *subjects* are usually separately studied. In natural learning, there is a complex interlocking connection of all the subjects. During play and other more studious forms of self-study, any number of subjects can be studied at any given time.

When a child is playing there are a great many *subjects* being studied in a natural way—from drama to music to science to math to language to history to art to psychology to biology to zoology to chemistry to athletics to physics to geography and so on.

Parents need to stop worrying about whether or not their children are learning all the institutional school's specified subjects, and start believing in their childrens' natural ability to learn.

Although it is remotely possible that a child could be stopped from learning, imagine to what lengths a parent would have to go to stop their child from learning. Think for a moment all the things your child/ren have learned that you would have rather they didn't: like climbing onto . . . ; opening up . . . ; running out of . . . ; and saying things . . . that were inappropriate.

There is much to learn in this life and children come with the *program* necessary to propel them towards the learning of every needful subject. This *program,* or *learning drive,* is composed of intellectual, social, emotional, physical, and spiritual facets that all search for expression.

In order to stop learning from happening, a child must be blocked from being able to express those facets of his or her person. The institutional school comes close to blocking almost all possibilities for expressing freely and learning naturally.

Consider *whole language:* Just as a baby understands language before verbalizing it, a child reads before writing. From *baby-tongue* to *mother-tongue.* Just as the baby first verbalizes in his or her *babinese* dialect and then evolves to the language spoken by those around him or her, the child first writes in his or her own *shorthand* and then evolves to the *spellings* of what he or she reads. Parents need only *speak* to their children in order for them to learn the language. Parallely, they need only *read* to their children that they may learn to read, and *write* for them that they may learn to write.

Consider *whole math:* Principles of math and mathematical concepts are automatically incorporated in real life learning situations. We measure, multiply, and divide while baking and cooking; and measure, calculate, and problem solve while designing and building. If children have measuring and calculating instruments (measuring tapes, cups and spoons, rulers, calculators, and weigh scales), available and accessible for their play and experimentation, they will be *absorbing* math. It is a *mathematical opportunity* for children to handle personal money (earnings or allowance) and keep a financial record or book in which earnings, savings, donations and spendings are recorded and, of course, calculated.

Consider *whole science:* Possible experiments are all around us. Experiments and observations are embarked upon when we: step into the bathtub (an experiment in volume displacement; *physics*); grow a garden (*biology*); bake breads and cakes (*chemistry*); star gaze (*astronomy*); or raise a puppy or kitten (*Zoology*). By *engaging in (safe) experiments,* children study, investigate, imagine, theorize, calculate, evaluate, measure, and observe. By *asking questions,* they make themselves scientists. What children do not ask questions? By *searching for answers,* he or she becomes a scientist. What child does not search for answers? When allowed to pursue their own interests, it is near, if not impossible, to prevent a child from becoming a scientist. Their inborn curiosity *demands* it of them. Parents simply must cooperate in and *guide* the process.

Consider *whole social sciences:* Give a child a globe and watch him or her roll into *geography.* Tell a child a story from the past and witness an *historical* search. Once children get going, they are difficult to stop, but who wants to? Turn on the news for your kids and you'll turn them on to *current affairs.* Children are very curious about the world around them, who else lives on it, and how we all fit into the global, historical, economical scheme of things. Parents must only guide, direct, and help their children find *sources* to the answers of their questions.

Consider *whole art:* In the words of Pablo Picasso (hate or love his art), "Every child is an artist. The problem is how to remain an artist once he grows up." If given the materials, from a simple pencil and paper, to a complex and expensive art studio full of paints, brushes, clay, and so forth; children will *blossom as artists.* (To avoid the mess children will surely manufacture if left alone, parents can get in the middle of master-piece making.) "Every artist was once an amateur" (Ralph Waldo Emerson), and every adult was once an artist. Parents need not *teach* the creative artist *out of* children like institutional schools tend to.

Consider *whole drama:* Children are *natural* actors. The spontaneity and free expression of children is unquestionable. Self-consciousness is alien to the natures of young children. *Playing is acting,* and acting is fun. Whether they *vicariously dramatize through* their *toy players* or get into the role of the character *personally,* they are *participating* in a *dramatic production.* While some productions are prepared and planned in fine and methodi-cal detail, others are totally impromtually ad-libbed. The whole family will benefit when parents play, too.

Consider *whole athletics:* Athletics come naturally to children. Kids *love* to walk, march, run, jump, squat, spring, bend, bounce, kick, lift, throw, catch, and climb in their comings and goings. Kids love to *play.* Kids can drive adults a little *crazy* with their seemingly *endless energy.* Organized competitive sports are unnecessary and less attractive to kids than *spontaneous sports.* Freestyle games *evolve according to need.* Exercise classes are unnecessary for free-flowing home schooled children but are needed for kids who are glued to a desk, in a class, in an institutional school all day.

Segmented subjects were originally derived out of *whole living* and *learning* as an attempt to categorize them. Life is an *intertwining experience* and is better enjoyed as a *whole* rather than in separated *parts.* More sense can be made out of something if one can see and feel the whole thing.

38) What do I do if my spouse isn't as enthusiastic as I am or, even worse, totally against it?

If your spouse is at least supportive, home schooling can work almost as well as when both parents are enthusiastic. You can share facts, theories, experiences and ideas about home schooling that will influence your partner. Your spouse can agree to read and research the subject of home schooling with an open mind and heart.

However, if your spouse is against home schooling, partially or totally, home schooling in your home will be hindered to whatever extent that this disagreeance causes problems. A house divided will not stand, so this division will need to be resolved. There must be some kind of agreed-upon terms for the home schooling effort to be successful.

When no compromise nor cooperative solutions can be reached between the partners who lead the household, the couple can't successfully work together as partners. Home schooling is often considered a moral issue. A few individuals believe that to home school their children is to provide a necessity for natural, healthy growth to adulthood. Some feel so strongly that they would even risk their marriage, if need be, to provide home schooling for their children. Like other far-reaching moral issues, home schooling has sometimes been the catalyst to a divorce.

In some cases, the home schooling advocative partner gives in to the other, who is anti-home schooling, in order to keep peace and to hold the family together. Those partners who *give in* and *give up* on what they really believe in betray themselves. Home schooling can be a very crucial decision to make. Those who favor it have strong opinions, as do those who oppose it.

Hopefully, you are in a marriage partnership where important long-term steps can be taken and destinations arrived at in a truly together fashion. Because the journey begins from differing origins does not mean that it must end that way.

In most cases, thankfully, the unwilling partner eventually comes around. If the marriage has a solid foundation, the home schooling choice would be just another divisive issue to be overcome. Mature, communicative couples will be able to work together to find a solution that is suitable to both of them.

39) I would like to work with the institutional schooling authorities. What steps should I take?

If you haven't already done so, contact a home schooling organization in your area in order to find out details that pertain to that particular area. There may be cooperative authorities, such as principals and superintendents, and favored approaches and alternatives.

Perhaps you could register with one of many correspondence schools (private and public). There are correspondence schools with programs especially geared to home schooling situations. Hopefully, the authorities in your area allow deviation from their *approved* curriculum.

Read up on home schooling experiences, where the family worked successfully with the institutional school system. Ask members of your local organization to share their positive experiences with you that you may glean some insight into whom to contact, what to ask for and how to do it.

You will likely be able to choose between the following options: write a carefully formulated *Letter of Intent to Home School,* explaining your reasons and plans to school on your own, and send it to the superintendent in your area; or contact and work closely or loosely with the principal of the school in your area by registering your child/ren there (you are the teacher, your child/ren the student/s, and your home the extended classroom); or work loosely with a principal from a distant school; utilize the *state* (*provincial*) correspondence program; or utilize a correspondence program of your choice.

Contact your school board regarding detailed legalities (school act and information/policies related to home schooling). You may need to pursue with passion, in order to discover all your rights and what you can demand. Ask around and realize you will be given false answers by those who are ignorant of the new, uncommon and continually changing policies.

Be aware that you are likely to be one of the numerous families who have experienced hassles and problems. More families are dissatisfied than satisfied with the way the institutional school system tends to deal with home schoolers. Read about those who have run into troubles and ask members of your home schooling group to share negative experiences they had while trying to work with the system, so that you may be forewarned of possible barriers and problems.

Once *registered in* the institutional school system, you may want to *get out* if you're unsatisfied or upset about your experiences with the authorities. When working with a principal, you can say that you are dissatisfied with the present arrangements and that you'll be looking for another *deal.* You can also say that you're *transferring* or *moving* to another school. The superintendent would need to know that you are *moving* out of that jurisdiction. Unfortunately, once you sign yourself *in,* it may be difficult to *get out* and you may actually need to move in order to *do it your way.*

(Donn Reed, in his *The Home School Challenge,* offers some interesting and useful tips to take advantage of when working with the authorities.)

40) I want to avoid the hassles and problems others have had working with the schooling authorities. How can I home school independent of the institutional school system?

If you are lucky enough to be considering home schooling before your children have reached institutional schooling registration age, you can prepare fully before the time arrives to actually implement your educational choice. You won't face the awkward task of removing your children from school.

If you have children in institutional school and you are bold and brave enough to begin home schooling immediately, there are a few popular ways to remove children from school in the middle of the school year. The most daring approach is to simply tell the principal of your intentions to home school.

Your superintendent has superiority over your principal, so if your principal is not cooperative you can try the superintendent in your area. (Your carefully formulated *Letter of Intent to Home School* could be modified and utilized for these purposes.) If your superintendent is not in favor of home schooling, you can *shop* around for the perfect principal or correspondence course elsewhere.

A more evasive approach is to announce your *transfer* to another school, a private school (your home school). You can claim that the new school will be sending for the records, but *you* won't be able to, because parents are not *allowed* to see the schooling records of their own children. (Sounds a little socialistic? It is!)

If your desire to try to home school independently just isn't quite enough to merit pulling your kids out of institutional school in the middle of the school year but the idea is haunting you, you could try calling them in sick for a couple of weeks. Most normal, healthy kids can always be counted on to be sick . . . sick of school! Taking a sudden holiday . . . a holiday from school would put your children out of school, too, for a few weeks!

Maybe you don't feel good about misleading the school authorities by fibbing. You can always read up on the subject now and wait until summer to begin the great experiment.

Many home schoolers begin their adventure after the institutional school is out for the summer holiday. You can say that you are moving, especially if you are! You can say that your children are changing to another school, a private school (your home school). You can just simply not re-register in the fall, and the absence of your children will likely go unnoticed.

If you get a call after the fall in regards to not having re-registered your child/ren, you can deal with that then. State/provincial school organizations move ever so slowly, like gargantuan ocean liners, so don't worry about impending harassment.

Even those parents who have phoned or written at the beginning of the school year to announce their intentions to home school often don't receive any response until well into the school year, and sometimes nearer the year end. You can always say that you're looking for the ideal program and that you're checking out all of the possibilities and alternatives. Parents often shop around for the perfect *deal* with a principal or superintendent for years.

If institutional schooling authorities *find* you and accuse you of harboring truants, disagree, insisting that your children are learning under your guidance just as many well-educated people have, past and present. Ask the authority to account for the many true truants—the children/kids who are in the streets and malls stealing, vandalizing, doing and dealing drugs, and getting into trouble of various kinds. Suggest that this authority would more wisely spend time and money (your tax dollars) providing help and guidance to the children whose parents don't provide thusly, rather than hassling parents such as yourself, who guide and nurture the learning of their children.

Should any authorities threaten to prosecute and take you to court, submit to only that which you must, stall as much as you can, evade when you can, and don't bend any more than is necessary. Check all possibilities. Make sure that you know your rights and the options that may be open to you.

Prepare to begin the new school year right . . . the way you choose to school your children, your own home school. Generations after you may thank heaven and you that you chose to accept the responsibility of educating your own children.

41) I'm home schooling and feeling unsure of myself. Any suggestions?

Now that your kids are home, you might begin to doubt your decision. Some parents do, some parents don't. It really is more a matter of confidence than a matter of skill. Kids actually can teach themselves. They need your supervision and your example. Be a parent—a provider, a protector, an example, a guide, a friend.

Remember that you have already home schooled your child/ren from their birth/s a little or a great deal, depending on you and your situation. How much did your child/ren learn at home under your guidance? To sit? To crawl? To walk? To talk? To read and write, even just a little? Look at how much you have accomplished!

The younger your children are when you begin, the better. If they are fortunate enough to have been spared from school or day-care, you likely have very healthy, normal children—children with self-esteem, healthy assertion, and loaded with a love for learning. Babies are born this way and nature intended them to remain so as they grow.

Children who have been force-fed information may not remember how to feed themselves, but the memories will return eventually. Relearn to love learning, yourself. That will be contagious. You won't be able to stop them from copying you. Their desire to learn will return.

The longer a child has been in an institutional school, the more withdrawal will be necessary. For some kids, it will be like an actual withdrawal sickness. They will have to recover from their dependency on being taught, instead of teaching themselves, as they once did. More withdrawal sickness will likely be witnessed, however, as they recover from their dependency on their peer group.

They may seem to do nothing for a while, but whether or not you recognize it they will be learning . . . something. Remember the *catch-up phenomenon*. Many home schooled children who have seemed slow for years have caught up and passed their same-aged peers in a couple of years. Many children don't move at all academically until twelve years of age and then they fly.

You can help them by providing interesting ideas of things to do and read. If you fill up your home with projects and books, eventually they'll just feel too hungry to pass it all up! More importantly, though, provide them with love and encouragement. Provide opportunities for growth in all aspects of their person.

Try not to put pressure on them to perform, as this will cause them to resist and retreat. Instead, focus on all the interesting things that you would like to do and read about. Your busyness in learning will catch fire with them. You'll be leading and they'll be following.

Don't *stage mother* them . . . get on the stage and start performing yourself! They'll want to join in on the act. Try not to forget that they need your guidance and help from time to time. You might get so busy that you practically ignore them entirely . . . but they'll still learn, anyway.

42) How will I explain to friends or family?

One of your greatest challenges just may be in dealing with well-intentioned friends and family. Learn to recognize between those who are genuinely interested in what you are doing and those who will be *concerned* all over you.

Try not to *hook in* to debates about differences in your educational beliefs. Contending about them won't do anyone any good. Agree to disagree. Allow them their narrow vision, if they choose to have it. Don't worry about those who don't agree with you.

A successful solution to the problem of spending hour upon hour explaining and defending your choice to others is simply to hand or mail information to those who inquire of you. A simple list of reading material, accompanied by a "Read up on the subject and we'll talk when you're finished," is sufficient. (Your carefully formulated *Letter of Intent to Home School* could be modified and utilized for these purposes.)

Some who just want to run your life will usually leave you alone after that. Some who are interested enough to read from your suggested list might just like what they've learned. Some who are too stubborn to see past their narrow education might come back for a fight, but you'll have had time to prepare another bunch of information for them to read.

43) Any ideas on how to evade inquisitions?

If you have chosen the most radical home schooling path to educate your child/ren independent of the schooling authorities, you may find sometimes that *silence is golden.* The majority of people will not be capable of accepting your choice as acceptable and you may not be capable of handling the insults, criticism and concerns that they may hand you, directly or indirectly.

Some people, particularly the *busy body, nosy neighbor, familiar family* types, will catch on pretty quickly that you're not taking the normal *send your kids off to the school* route. When they begin to ask, inquire or quiz you and your child/ren about what on earth you're up to, you'd be wise to have prepared some quick answers and comeback questions.

As a family, you can discuss the possible *hurdles of questions* that you'll likely come up against, and you'll be able to *jump them with ease* when and if the time comes. Two basic formulas you may make use of for responding to inquiries are: to answer in general terms and to answer with another question.

It might be a good idea to turn the attention of the question away from you and your family by taking your answer or question-answer in another direction. You don't have to give your opinion or tell what you are doing. Instead, you can give a general home schooler's opinion, an expert's opinion or tell what other home schoolers are doing.

You can keep control of the line of questioning by staying assertively on your toes. If you need assertiveness training, practice within your family in role-play situations. To find possible answers to each possible inquiry, keep in mind two things: should we answer with a general answer or should we answer with another question.

Some general answers might begin as follows: Most home schoolers do . . . ; Some home schoolers try . . . ; The average home schooling parent thinks that . . . ; Ask my mom or dad about that . . . ; My mom has some stuff you can read . . . ; My dad could tell you all about it . . . ; If you are interested in home schooling, you can . . . ; I can give you some material about home schooling to read . . . ; After you have read up on the subject . . . ; There are a number of theories about that . . . ; There are many ways to home school, such as . . . ; There are experts who have found that . . . ; You'd be surprised how many home schoolers. . . .

Some question-answers are as follows: How did you *find out* we were home schooling? Haven't you heard about home schooling, *yet?* What do *you* know about home schooling? Are you interested in home schooling, *too?* Would you like some *reading material* on the subject? Do you want a *list of books* to read? Aren't you worried about the *anti-socialization* your kids are getting at institutional school? How much computer time do *you* (or *your kids*) get at school? How are *your* kids doing in their schooling? Aren't you worried about all the *violence, sex, and drugs* at the schools? Do you realize how *long* home schooling has been around? Don't you (or your kids) *hate* sitting in a hard desk all day? Did you know that there are more and more families home schooling *every year?* Do you think testing *helps,* and *why?*

You'll probably find the constant questioning far more tiresome than what any of the educational responsibilities could ever be. The bombardment of questions and reactions at the beginning will die down eventually, at least to a dull roar. This will pass.

Your children will likely find that the initial response from their friends is of the "wow, neato, I wish I could do that" type. After the friends beg their parents to do it too, run head on into the "no way, what a stupid thing to do" wall, they'll be back with all the reasons your kids shouldn't dare to home school. This, too, will pass.

The curiosity, shock, or horror that friends, family, or neighbors may display upon discovering your educational choice will eventually dissipate. They'll all get used to the idea in a short time. Gossip will die down. Your new life-style won't seem quite so newsy in a while. When the next interesting bit of news flies by, you'll be all but forgotten. *Focus in* towards your family for the next little while, rather than *focussing out* towards the thoughts and words of others. Concentrate on home schooling.

44) Is it possible, in order to avoid all the possible problems, to home school without anyone knowing that you are involved in doing it?

There are those who feel they need to *quietly* home school and they keep silent about what they have chosen to do. They know that they don't want the opposition—the criticism, contention, coercion and even *crucifying* — that may inevitably follow should they go *public* with their chosen educational practices.

Some feel justified in hiding the truth from any possible *enemy*. They evade and avoid questions and mislead with their evasive and elusive answers and statements about their childrens' schooling. Some keep their children *in* the home during institutional school hours to avoid suspicion. Dependent upon the situation, these families do and say varied things to protect themselves from interference in the education of their children.

There are many families who pursue this course, the one of least resistance; so you are not alone in considering it. You can covertly home school for years (many families have), depending on how intimate your social activity with family, friends, and neighbors is.

Since those who choose home schooling tend to be individualists, they often already pursue somewhat self-propelled life-styles. Whether it is the overt anti-home schooling words and actions of others that drive them into a protective covert stance, or just that they tend towards their own protectionism, it all depends on the family in question.

If you feel that this is your *best bet*, give it a *spin;* you can't lose. You can always tell people what you're up to later if you change your mind.

Some independent home schooling parents employ a *linguistic facade* when explaining the schooling situation of their children to others. They say things like, "Our child/ren are enrolled in a special *pilot project,* where they study predominantly *off campus,* under our *tutorial guidance.*" Or, "Our child/ren are taking part of an *independent research and study program,* along with many other gifted students." Most people respond with, "Oh!" What else can they say. If they think that your children have been chosen by schooling professionals for these special educational alternatives, they are satisfied.

45) Are their any primary individuals to thank for the resurgence of home schooling?

Holt and Moore are two names that come to mind for many home schoolers as champions for this cause:

John Holt wrote a number of books and spoke a great deal on or relative to the subject of home schooling. He was the founder of *Growing Without Schooling* (G.W.S.), a worldwide newsletter for home schooling families and advocates. Many home schoolers mourned his relatively recent passing, and although his words still persist, they miss his direct influence.

Raymond and Dorothy Moore have been furthering home schooling for many years as well. They have also written a number of books and speak often about home schooling and related topics. The Moores continue the fight for home schooling rights, and numerous home schoolers are grateful that they do.

There are other individuals who are grabbing hold of the home schooling torch, although none have reached a status of national prominence yet. Some are leading on local levels, while others are spreading their influence regionally and nationally. Once *in* the home schooling *community*, the growing number of names of these *champions for the cause* will become increasingly apparent to you.

46) What can I do to help win the freedoms in education that home schooling advocates hope for?

Write, write, write . . . letters to your government representatives, after you have read enough to formulate your personal beliefs on the matter of educational and general freedoms. Share what you have come to know with others that more of the general public may be aware of this positive educational alternative. (Your carefully formulated *Letter of Intent to Home School* could be modified and utilized for these purposes.)

The more parents who manage to properly educate their children according to their own consciences, the more home schooling will be able to prove itself. The greatest barriers to *managing to properly educate* children are interference and intervention of institutional schooling's authorities.

Some home schoolers believe in the cause enough that they donate time, energy, and money towards the promoting of it. Simple advertisements are placed in local newsletters and papers, and brochures explaining basic home schooling information are planted in stores and libraries.

Forming or joining local and regional home schooling organizations can help to further the cause. By being in touch with the latest trends and policies, you'll be better equipped to know what you can do for your family and others in general. The *strength* that comes from *numbers* will also aid in the cause, particularly for political lobbying.

As greater numbers of home schooling success stories permeate society, the freedoms of parents in educating their own children will more easily be won.

47) For those children who remain in institutional schools, what can be done to promote more real learning?

The more an institutional school could look and behave like a home, the better. The schooling authorities would do well to first cooperate with home schooling families and then look to them for examples to follow.

Those families working with the schooling authorities need much more *elbow room* in order to allow more real learning to take place. Once institutional schooling authorities grant home schooling parents the autonomy that is rightfully theirs, independent home schoolers will begin to come out of the *woodwork*, the *closet*, and out from the *underground*.

The *survival of the fittest* principle applies to learning enhancement methods, and those methods which aid learning the most will survive only when nature is allowed to take its rightful course. Those home schooling parents who have secured *total autonomy* are discovering the most successful *methods*.

By exercising autonomy in parental responsibilities, including teaching, guiding, and learning, the parent is free to choose those *things* which *feel right*. Although there are those who would argue that parents should not be allowed to raise their children in such a haphazard fashion, there are those parents who claim that it is their basic right to do so.

The vast majority of home schools are places where creative and productive learning is happening. Most home schooling situations work. The vast majority of institutional schools are places where creativity and desire to learn is being slaughtered. Most institutional schooling situations don't work.

If institutional schooling authorities were to get down off of their usurped thrones and put all parents back in their rightful place as rulers in the educational choices of their own children, public education systems could begin to evolve toward something more natural and efficient. Parents could help make sure their own kids were getting their best chance at learning.

The parent-teacher organizations, often *glorified appendages* of schools, aren't much more than *busywork* organizations. Involvement in the PTA often distracts parents from their educational responsibility to their children. The institutional public school was *created to serve families,* but *families now serve the public school system.*

If the PTA was given greater power than the school board of authorities, some positive changes might occur. If public schools were turned over to private industry, improvements would almost be certain. Every child's right to an education need not be forgotten if financial help for education were given to those who need it.

The three thousand plus dollars (the amount depends on each area's governmental allotments) generally used per child per year for the educating of children in public schools could be more wisely used by parents. Some school reformers suggest a voucher system, whereby each family would receive educational vouchers which could be used to *buy* the *educational programs* and *products of their choice.* There are those who have tried to change and improve the schools. Caring teachers and educational researchers and experts have pushed hard for much needed changes and improvements but to little avail.

Many champions of school reform have given up on institutional schools and have begun to promote home schools. The barriers to school reform may be rooted in politics—politics of the *state* and/or politics of the *institutional school.*

48) Why did you decide to home school?

Our home schooling trek did not begin after my first brief introduction to it (home schoolers were sharing their choice on the "Donahue" show, early in 1978), largely because I did not know where to begin or if I was capable of doing so. Six years later, when I knew a few families who began home schooling, I started to ask questions.

A pivotal point in my having been convinced about home schooling was having listened to an audio cassette tape of a speech given by Reed A. Benson. (This tape can be purchased through the non-profit organization, the *National Center for Constitutional Studies.*) It left me *drop-jaw amazed*, a *tear-stained believer*, and *race-poised ready*, and I fervently desired to embark as a pioneer on the home schooling path. Like seeing a light at the end of a tunnel, it took only a matter of minutes before I knew there was no turning back. We had to do it, as we could not ignore the strong feelings and conviction that had suddenly become a part of us.

I decided to search further for answers to the many questions that I had. After reading about and personally seeing positive effects of home schooling upon children, I began to recognize damages which had been inflicted upon our eldest child by the institutional school for two years. It was like I had just come out of a *thick fog* and could now see *clearly*.

It was difficult to allow our son to finish the last couple of months of institutional schooling (prior to the summer holidays). It seemed hypocritical, considering what we had discovered.

We believed, when we began that we were offering our children the best all-round education possible. We still believe that. The longer we home school our children, the more we know there is no better way to educate our kids.

In order to illustrate our home schooling philosophy, let me share with you our general *Letter of Intent to Home School* that I wrote to send to the institutional schooling authorities:

> Dear Mr. or Ms. Schooling Official:
> At the commencement of this new school year, I forward this letter to you in regards to our children who reside with us, in your jurisdiction. This letter is to inform you that we have chosen

an alternative form of education and will be home schooling our children, rather than partaking of the public school offering.

If you are not already acquainted with the home schooling renaissance, perhaps you would like to familiarize yourself with some of the many books about home schooling and related subjects. I am enclosing a reading list that may be of interest to you. At least hundreds of thousands of known home schoolers continually add to the data and reading material on the subject. Including families unregistered with institutional schools, researchers estimate that there are actually more than a million home schoolers in North America. Of those families who school independently of and unregistered with the institutional schools, some work overtly (sometimes labeled *independent* home schoolers) and others work covertly (often labeled *closet* or *underground* home schoolers).

Our reasons for choosing the home schooling approach are vast and varied, but I will try to briefly summarize so that you may come to a general understanding of our position. We feel certain that our children can benefit greatly by learning under our loving guidance and care. As parents to our children, we accept the responsibility that we feel is ours first; to raise them by nurturing, instructing, and guiding them towards adulthood. We believe that we are qualified to provide *sufficient instruction* to our children, based out of our home, while utilizing every educational avenue available to us in and around our community.

The curriculum our children will follow could be described as natural or whole learning, otherwise known as holistic education. You may already be aware of this newly renewed approach to learning, which is beginning to permeate the institutional schools, after being practiced for many years in home schools throughout the world. However, if you have not yet heard about holistic learning, we recommend that you seek out information on this philosophy.

Subjects that are covered in the institutional school setting will be covered by our children. However, we will employ an integrative whole subject approach, rather than a fragmented lesson method as is common in the public school. All areas of academic, artistic, and athletic fields will be explored, intertwined in the daily lives of our children. Their social development will be enhanced by the many-faceted relationships that they will have available to them; through association with a variety of people of differing ages, races, and creeds.

Our children will not need to be tested, as we will be evaluating their progress on an ongoing basis. We strongly oppose testing, as we consider it counterproductive, particularly in conjunction with the self-directed holistic learning method, which we will incorporate. We have every confidence that our children will continue to learn at an energetic pace as they have previously done to date.

We trust that you will grant us the freedom to exercise our inherent right to assume the responsibility of educating our own children. If your assistance is required in relation to our children's educational needs, we will contact you. Thank you for your time, attention, and cooperation.

Respectfully yours,
(Ted and) Kerri Bennett Williamson

49) Would you recommend home schooling for every family?

I, personally, would recommend home schooling to every family that can find a way to do so. This is simply because I believe in home schooling with all my heart. Upon reading this, I know that there are many who would disagree with me.

"What possible *proof* do you have that home schooling could be recommended for *every* family" they may ask. I have seen enough *proof* to convince me that home schooling is the most natural and logical method of learning.

I have seen the good it can do. I have seen troubled children turn around after leaving institutional schools and after beginning home schooling. I have seen home schooling make happy children out of institutional schools' unhappy children.

Unfortunately, I have also seen the destruction that the institutional school can cause in children's lives. I can see how institutional school hurt me. I can see how much I missed out on during my institutional school years. I can't go back to then, but I've been home schooling myself ever since I left that big brick building. I am determined to give my children what I wish I could have had: home schooling.

All basically good parents are capable of home schooling their children, if they so desire. *Where there is a will there is a way,* but the key word is *will,* or *desire.* Every family who is willing to make the effort can take advantage of some or all of the benefits of home schooling.

It need not be *proven* that home schooling is the best place to start when educating children, to make it true. Many of us believe that *feeling* that something is true is sufficient proof. Known to many as *conscience, instinct, intuition, inspiration, discernment, gut feelings,* and so forth, following the words of one's heart is enough proof of truth. As *scientifically proven data* can be later proven wrong or inaccurate, it is unwise to worship that which is seemingly proven.

Some day in the not so distant future, maybe this naturally superior form of schooling will be readily available to all families. Home schooling advocates usually agree that this would do much to cure many of society's ills.

Some home schooling parents hope and feel, as Reed A. Benson does, "Perhaps the classroom of tomorrow will be the family living room."

50) What can I read to learn more about home schooling?

I recommend John Holt's *Teach Your Own, How Children Learn,* and *The Home Schooling Resource List;* Raymond and Dorothy Moore's *School Can Wait, Home-Style Teaching,* and *Hewitt Research Foundation;* and Frank Smith's *Insult To Intelligence* as the best places to start in your search for more in-depth information in the area of home schooling.

Although no one source can guarantee all truth and all the answers, there is much that can be gleaned from many sources. Research with an open mind and heart, following your own conscience. Only you can decide what you believe.

Periodicals/organizations that are commonly recommended by home schoolers are listed as follows:

GROWING WITHOUT SCHOOLING (newsletter) and The Home Schooling Resource List
729 Boylston St., Boston MA, 02116

EDUCATION OTHERWISE (newsletter)
25 Common Lane, Hemmingford Abbots,
Cambridgeshire, PE18 9AN

HEWITT RESEARCH FOUNDATION
P.O. Box 9, Washougal, WA 98671

THE HOME SCHOOL LEGAL DEFENSE ASSOCIATION
Box 2091, Washington, DC 20013

NATIONAL CENTER FOR CONSTITUTIONAL STUDIES
P.O. Box 37110, Washington DC 20013

Many home schooling advocates often recommend the following authors/books relevant to home schooling, education, and learning:

ARMSTRONG, Thomas
In Their Own Way. Los Angeles: J.P. Tarcher, 1987.

ASHTON-WARNER, Sylvia
Teacher. New York: Simon and Schuster, 1963.

BARBE, Walter Burke
Growing up Learning. Washington DC: Acropolis, 1985.

BECK, Joan Wagner
How to Raise a Brighter Child. New York: Pocket Books, 1975.

BERGMAN, Mary and Tom
Survival Family: Hawkes Publishing, Inc., 1977.

COHEN, Howard
Equal Rights For Children. Totowa NJ: Rowman and Littlefield, 1980.

COLFAX, David and Micki
Home Schooling for Excellence. Mountain House Press, 1987.

CROALL, Jonathan
Neill of Summerhill. New York: Pantheon Books, 1983.

CROSBY, Nina
Don't Teach, Let Me Learn. Buffalo NY: D.O.K. Publishers, 1980.

DOMAN, Glenn
How To Teach Your Baby To Read. Philadelphia: Better Baby Press, 1979.
Teach Your Baby Math. New York: Pocket Books, 1982.
How To Multiply Your Baby's Intelligence. Garden City, NY: Doubleday, 1984.

ELKIND, David
Child Development and Education. New York: Oxford University Press, 1976.
The Child and Society. New York: Oxford University Press, 1979.
The Hurried Child. Reading, MA: Addison-Wesley, 1981.
All Grown Up & No Place To Go. Reading, MA: Addison-Wesley, 1984.
Miseducation: Preschoolers at Risk. New York: Knopf, 1987.

GOERTZEL, Victor and Mildred G.
Cradles of Eminence. Boston: Little, Brown, 1962.

GRAUBARD, Allen
Free the Children. New York: Pantheon Books, 1972.

HANSON, Jeanne K.
Game Plans for Children. New York: Putnam, 1981.

HOLT, John
Teach Your Own. New York: Delacorte Press/Seymour Lawrence, 1981.
How Children Learn. New York: Delacorte Press/Seymour Lawrence, 1983.
How Children Fail. New York: Delacorte Press/Seymour Lawrence, 1982.
Instead of Education. New York: E.P. Dutton, 1976.
The Underachieving School: New York: Pitman Pub. Corp., 1969.
What Do I Do Monday? New York: Dutton, 1970.
Never Too Late. New York: Delacorte Press, 1978.
Freedom and Beyond. New York: E.P. Dutton, 1972.

ILLICH, Ivan
Deschooling Society. New York: Harper & Row, 1971.

JENKINS, Mollie
School Without Tears. London: Collins, 1973.

JOUDRY, Patricia
And The Children Played. Montreal: Plattsburgh NY: Tundra Books, 1975.

LEDSON, Sidney
Raising Brighter Children: New York: Walker and Co., 1987.

LEWIS, Terry
Schools on Trial: Christian School Consultants, 1985.

MARZOLLO, Jean
Supertot: creative learning activities for children. New York: Harper & Row, 1977

McCURDY, Harold G.
The Childhood Pattern of Genius: Horizon, 1960.

MELTON, David
How to Help Your Preschooler Learn More. New York: D. McKay Co., 1976.

MOORE, Raymond and Dorothy
Better Late Than Early. New York: Reader's Digest Press, 1975.
School Can Wait. Provo, UT: Brigham Young University Press, 1979.
Home Grown Kids. Waco TX: Word Books, 1981.
Home Spun Schools. Waco TX: Word Books, 1982.
Home Style Teaching.

ORLIC, Terry
Every Kid Can Win. Chicago: Nelson-Hall Co., 1975.

PRIDE, Mary
The Big Book of Home Learning. Good News, 1986.
The Next Book of Home Learning. Good News, 1987.
The New Big Book of Home Learning. Good News, 1988.
Schoolproof. Good News, 1988.
Turn Your Heart Toward Home

RASBERRY, Salli
How to Start Your Own School. California: Freestone Pub. Co., 1970

REED, Donn
The Home-School Challenge. Glassville, NB: Brook Farm Books, 1985.
The First Home-School Catalogue. Glassville, NB: Brook Farm Books, 1986.

SMITH, Frank
Insult to Intelligence. New York: Arbor House, 1986.
Reading. London; New York: Cambridge University Press, 1978.
Understanding Reading. New York: Toronto: Rinehart and Winston, 1978.
Writing and the Writer. New York: Holt, Rinehart, and Winston, 1982.

SONNIER, Isadore L.
Methods and Techniques of Holistic Education. Springfield, IL: C.C. Thomas, 1985.
Holistic Education: Teaching-Learning ... Philos Lib, 1982

TRUE, Michael
Homemade Social Justice. Chicago IL: Fides/Claretian, 1982.

Wallace, Nancy
Better Than School. Burdett, NY: Larson, 1983.

Williams, Emily Needham
High Tech Babies: An Owner's Manual. Dallas TX: Pressworks, 1986.

TOPICAL GUIDE

Topics: Question Numbers

Academics: 10, 13–15, 17, 19–23
Anti-socialization: 7, 43
Apprenticeship: 14
Arts: 11, 19, 23
Athletics: 11, 23
Attendance: 14, 27
Behavior: 7–9, 13, 15, 16, 19, 21, 22, 26, 28
Boredom: 13, 16, 36
Catch-up phenomenon: 19, 21, 23
Censoring: 6
Closet/underground home schoolers: 17, 35, 47
Computers: 12, 18, 43
Curriculum: 4, 6, 17, 36, 37
Creativity: 6–9, 13, 15, 19, 23, 47
Daily regimen: 27
Drugs: 4, 8, 40, 43
Early entrance: 23, 24
Educational guiding: 14, 19, 23, 36, 47
Experimentation: 6, 37
Explaining: 42, 43, 44
Failure: 19–22
Famous home schoolers: 10, 11
Fractional (fragmented) bit learning: 20–22
Freedom fighting: 3, 45, 46
Generation gap: 5, 26
Genius: 6, 10, 15, 19, 22, 23
Government intervention: 3, 6, 7, 23, 24, 31
Guinea pigs: 6
Health: 8, 23
History: 2, 15, 24
Holistic education: 14, 15, 18, 19, 23, 28, 37, 48
How to: 34, 35, 36, 37, 41, 42
Hyperactivity: 8

INDIVIDUALS QUOTED OR MENTIONED

Individuals: Question Numbers

ADAMS, John Quincy: 11
ANDERSEN, Hans Christian: 10
BELL, Alexander Graham: 10
BENSON, Ezra Taft: 6, 9
BENSON, Reed A.: 6, 13, 14, 49
BURROUGHS, John: 11
CARNEGIE, Andrew: 11
CHAPLIN, Charles: 11
CHRISTIE, Agatha: 10
CHURCHILL, Sir Winston: 11
CLARK, George Rogers: 11
COOKE, Edmund Vance: 28
COWARD, Noel: 11
DA VINCI, Leonardo: 11
DICKENS, Charles: 10
DOMAN, Glenn: 14
DRIER, Thomas: 13
EDISON, Thomas: 10, 17
EINSTEIN, Albert: 16, 19
EMERSON, Ralph Waldo: 37
FEYNMAN, Richard: 17
FRANKLIN, Benjamin: 11
GANDHI, M.K.: 23
HAZLITT, William: 10
HOLMS, Oliver Wendell: 17
HOLT, John: 1, 7, 14, 19
HUGO, Victor: 9
ILLICH, Ivan: 16
KAPLOWE, Joseph K.: 17
KETTERING, Charles Franklin: 10
LEWIS, C.S.: 10
LINCOLN, Abraham: 11
MCDONALD, Bob: 15
MARX, Karl: 6